Ronin Robot Press
Rock Creek Consulting, LLC
9715 Holmhurst Road
Bethesda MD 20817
©2016 Cyd Andrews-Looper All rights reserved.
TWO PEWS FROM CRAZY is a
RONIN ROBOT PRESS publication.

TWO PEWS FROM CRAZY

My Insane Journey from Christian Fundamentalism to a Faith of Love Alone— LGBTQ Minister

BY

REV. CYD ANDREWS-LOOPER

ENDORSEMENTS

"It has been said that the best way to write is to sit down at the keyboard and open a vein. This incarnational gift packaged as a book, "*Two Pews from Crazy*", is the courageous result of just that —the opening of a vein. Read it in doses with space between readings to reflect on the life hidden in the veins of your own soul. Perhaps, and hopefully, you will be inspired to do your own opening, if only for yourself."

Rev. Stan Mitchell,
Sr. Pastor, GracePointe Church, Franklin, TN

"In *Two Pews from Crazy* the author takes us on a painful but always hopeful spiritual journey that made me think of Pilgrim's Progress. Each time this lesbian Christian pastor nears the 'Celestial City,' there's another 'Slough of Despond,' 'Valley of Humiliation' or 'River of Death' to cross. It's a kind of miracle that Rev. Cyd is still standing after being born a female in a male dominated culture, after accepting her sexual orientation in the homophobic South, after refusing to renounce her call to ministry in a Christian community that forbids women clergy, after adopting a child, losing three different partners, and suffering through spiritual and emotional abuse as a pastor.

"Cyd has a great sense of humor. The chapters are short. Her story is honest, frank, easy to follow and never dull. And though her journey is sometimes painful to read, it is also a celebration of God's presence and power in the life of a lesbian, Christian pastor who never stops believing that God loves her and is with her every step of the way. Reading Cyd's story reminded me that God loves me, too, and is with me on my own sometimes painful journey.

"If you need to be reminded of the Holy Spirit's presence and power in your life, just sit down next to Rev. Cyd just *Two Pews from Crazy* and enjoy."

Mel White,
Author, Stranger at the Gate: To be Gay and Christian in
America

Table of Contents

DEDICATIONS
This book is dedicated to my Earthly Angels:

Angie Dittrich

Angie, thank you for your presence, your love, your prayers, your hugs…your willingness to step into my "fishbowl world" and make me feel so safe. You were a gift from God. God allowed our paths to cross for a season. Be blessed on your journey!

Sally Thornton Gore & Karen Pryor

You have become family to me. Your love, emotional, spiritual and financial support have given me new hope that I thought I would never find. Thank you for believing in me when I could not believe in myself. Thank you for constantly covering me in protective light. I want to make you proud!

Laurie Beriswell & Lee Ann Pagel

You girls have given me love, courage and financial support in the darkest part of my journey. Thank you for your light and generous hearts. Your faces still bring me such joy!

Dave & Rodney Damron

You guys are like brothers to me. The safe space, listening ears, huge hugs and hearts that enveloped me gave me the ability to see beyond the darkness. You also gave so generously of your finances to help me live through the dark and barren months of this journey.

Amanda Collins & Beth Nielsen Jimmy James

Thank you, sincerely, for your financial support! May you be blessed as you so generously bless those around you!

My Holy Trinity-Nashville Family

You will never know how much I love you! I trust that this book answers some of the questions that have been in your hearts. I birthed you and you will always be like a child to me. I love you and pray often for you. May God continue to bless you as you follow Christ and live out His love and light in Nashville. I remind you as I have reminded you many times, there's nothing you can do to make God love you more; and, there's nothing you can do to make God love you less. God loves you just as you are!

Never forget that!!

My GracePointe Church Family

Stan, Melissa, Paul, Ron, Carol, Kimberly, Justin, Keri, Rachel, August, Jason … and so many others. Thank you for your love. Thank you for the safe places you gave me that allowed me to begin my journey of healing! I am so proud to call you family! I am so proud of who you have become and the amazing light you are shining forth to the world!

My Holy Trinity-Memphis Church Family

You will never know how God has used you to bring continued healing to my soul and spirit. You will always be close to my heart.

My Fellow Bearers of Light:

Brody Taylor, Gretchen Bryant, Alison Langley, The Ray Family, Jim Hennessey, Toby West, Kara Porter, Sascha David, David Nalls, Rick Self, Debbie Ottarski, Catherine Franco, Penny & Jiles Wanna, Erin Hardiman & Haley Baird, Judy Berryhill, Julie McIntyre, Katie Lockhart, Jean Eaton, Jeff Myrick, Carrie Brown, Alice Crafts, Laura Wellington, Allison Clark, Zach Valder, Heather Cavaliere, Kim & Beth Thompon, Kathy Pack & Melissa Friend, Rita White & Lesa Mears, Anita Manning, Timothy Oldham, Michael Neely, Jason Prentice, Sheri Conn, Carlene Dickinson, Christa Cruikshank, Robert Leaman, Brandi Kristi, Rachel Kihn, Kim & Nancy Mills, Carol Brusegar, David Nalls, Brandi Grizzard-Snead, J. Read Hodge, Kelly & Bene' Simpson-Ruiz, Melissa Laster, Todd Liebergen, Joyce McCown, & Kevin Jaskulski.

INTRODUCTION

November 2014

I am in the midst of transition as I type these words. A month ago, I left an eighteen-year ministry as pastor of Holy Trinity Community Church in Nashville, Tennessee. I started a small Bible study in the fall of 1996, not knowing it would eventually grow into an amazing congregation representing God's wonderful diversity. Since 2005, I have served as full-time pastor and spiritual shepherd to an open and affirming congregation whose arms are open to anyone who enters—men, women, children and youth, straight, gay, lesbian, bisexual, transgender, black, white, Latino, Asian, former Baptist, Pentecostal, Church of Christ, Methodist, Presbyterian, Lutheran, Catholic, Episcopal … the list goes on and on. The congregation grew from a small Bible study of ten to twelve people to a congregation of more than 700. As difficult as it was to leave this congregation, I know beyond a shadow of a doubt that my work at Holy Trinity is finished and that God is leading me to a new chapter in my life and ministry.

I have had several books brewing within my spirit for a number of years now. I actually started writing one of them within the last month when God said, "You need to tell your story first." So it is from that place of obedience that I write this book.

I don't know about you, but I have never thought of my life or story as extraordinary. I have experienced successes and losses like everyone else, but I don't consider what I have faced to be anything to write home about. It wasn't until some dear friends pointed out some of the unique elements of my faith, background and story in which I began to believe that, perhaps, others could find hope in me telling it. Where I am today in my faith and where I was in my teenage years and early adulthood are drastically different. I have gone to places my childhood faith told me I could not and should not go. And, for many years, I lived in the shame, fear, and insanity of my strict Baptist upbringing. But as you journey with me through my story, you will see how I found amazing peace and hope by understanding and embracing the highest love we can experience as human beings. You will see how God used me—a simple girl raised on a chicken farm in South Carolina—to communicate love to hundreds of souls who had lost hope.

You will journey with me as I embrace my call to ministry as a woman—something the church in which I grew up saw as sinful. You will walk with me as I face my sexual orientation—something I believed would damn my soul to hell for eternity. You will follow me through some of my lowest points—through losses that made me long for death. But you will also see me overcome life's many challenges, obstacles, and valleys through my faith. You will see the abundant blessings God has brought into my life. You will see how God can and will use your life and bring you to your purpose, if you will simply embrace your identity as a child of God and live from that authentic place. If you were raised in conservative or fundamentalist Christianity, are a woman in ministry, are part of the LGBTQ community and have struggled with your faith and orientation, had weight issues that affected your health, been responsible for making difficult decisions for an aging parent, or experienced spiritual and emotional abuse as a pastor, you will connect with my story.

I don't share my story with the idea that I have all the answers. I share it in hopes that some part of it resonates with you. I share it in hopes that you, too, will find new hope in your faith journey, no matter the situation. My life has been characterized, as it is even now, by blind faith, as again and again I step out into the unknown with God and see God open doors and unfold blessings that I could never imagine.

Come, journey with me and find your hope again....

Rev. Cyd Andrews-Looper

CHAPTER 1

Nothing Fun About Fundamentalism

My family life as a child included a strong, conservative Christian influence. My parents were members of the Tabernacle Baptist Church in Greenville, South Carolina. It was an "independent, Bible-believing Baptist Church" that had broken away from the Southern Baptist Church in the late '50s because of the "growing presence of liberalism." The hallmark of this church was its strong fundamentalist Christian doctrines. The only Bible translation allowed was the King James Version (Scofield Bible). The Bible was seen as infallible and inerrant. Every word of Scripture was believed to have been literally inspired by God; and anyone who challenged or questioned this belief was labeled as liberal and heretical.

The extreme fundamentalist approach to Scripture was played out in the church's rigid gender roles. The specific roles assigned to men and women were thought to be ordained by God. Men were to provide the leadership and final authority in matters of the church and home. Women were to be in subservient roles to men. In all my years growing up in this fundamentalist church, I never once saw a woman lead prayer in public. Women were taught to "keep silent in church." They were allowed to teach children through age seven. After that age, boys and girls were separated and the men taught the boys.

Because of the literal interpretation of the New Testament scriptures, women were not allowed to wear pants or anything that was considered "men's apparel." Men were expected to keep their hair short.

My parents were a bit more practical in administering this expectation. Wearing dresses on the farm could actually be dangerous. With the climbing, pulling and being around farm machinery, it was important to wear clothing that was comfortable and allowed ease of movement. It was simply impractical to wear dresses while working on the farm. There were other issues my parents saw as somewhat impractical, like prohibition of television and avoidance of "mixed bathing" (men & women) at the pool. In general, my parents were quite conservative in their Christian faith, but I found them to be somewhat practical in their choices to live it out.

I remember my dad often saying, "Lord willing"—it used to irritate me that he always thought everything he did had to be "the Lord's will." I remember seeing my dad and mom reading their Bibles each night before going to bed and praying together as well. My dad would always take his bath, put on his pajamas and then tune in to the local Christian radio station that played the southern gospel music he loved to hear.

A fond memory I have is lying beside him listening to southern gospel music before going to bed each night. Sometimes he would sing along with the songs—which was funny to me—Dad didn't have a singing voice. Other times he would say "amen" after a song and tell me what truth he was agreeing with. I saw in my dad and mom a dependence on God in their everyday life. I believe this was one of the greatest gifts my parents gave me and an important lesson in my personal journey of faith.

The faith I saw my parents live made me feel safe and loved; yet the beliefs and practices of the church we attended seemed distant and impractical. The only reason I am aware of that my parents stayed in this church was that they loved to hear Dr. Harold B. Sightler preach. My parents grew in their personal faith because of the truths they came to understand about God's plan of salvation. While I always thought the other people in the church were rigid and a bit weird, I nevertheless gained valuable truth and insights about God. I became a Christian at sixteen and was baptized by Dr. Sightler, a man of great physical and spiritual stature to me. Sixteen was older than the age of most youth taking this big life step. I think there are several reasons why I didn't do it earlier. First, I never really felt connected to the youth that were my age. While we attended church every time the doors were open, we didn't socialize with other families; mainly because we lived almost 45 minutes from the church. Second, this was a church of over 4000 people. The thought of stepping out into the aisle while the choir sang "Just As I Am," was petrifying to me. It wasn't until the summer of 1978 in which Dr. Sightler was preaching through the book of Revelation on Sunday nights that I got the "hell scared out of me"…and asked my Daddy to walk down the aisle with me. I did not want to go to hell. The conviction I felt became overwhelming. That first step into the aisle was the hardest, but it also brought the most peace. A couple of weeks later I was baptized by Dr. Sightler. I remember feeling very safe spiritually when he baptized me. So, despite the fundamentalist, conservative influence the church had in my life, I find myself thankful for the element of spiritual safeness it brought to me as a youth. A core belief of Baptist theology is eternal security or "once saved, always saved." Embracing the faith brought comfort to my soul at a young age. There are passages of scripture which I can quote from memory because I heard them so often from the pulpit. Sometimes this was good—if the passage spoke of God's mercy or grace. Other times, it was a spiritual nightmare—such as when the passage told me I was going to hell for being "different."

What I found especially difficult about growing up in this conservative church were the expectations they had for me as a woman. If I chose to participate in any activity with the youth, I had to wear a skirt or gauchos. I cannot begin to describe how I abhorred this apparel. I was, from a young age, quite a tomboy. I helped my dad around the farm and wore jeans and tennis shoes. I went fishing with my dad and wore jeans and tennis shoes. I played softball for a local Southern Baptist Church (SBC was considered liberal by my home church) and wore jeans and tennis shoes. Yet, when I went to activities sponsored by my home church, I had to be something I wasn't and dress in a way that was very uncomfortable and inauthentic. When I talked to my parents about it, they acknowledged that the dress code was rigid; but they simply said I needed to "abide by the rules" if I wanted to participate. It did not take me long to decide that it was not worth participating. These "Christian standards" seemed ridiculous. Never had I felt that God wanted me to wear dresses or, God forbid—gauchos…OMG! It really made no sense to me. Over time, these Christian standards made me somehow feel less than a "real" Christian. At every turn, there seemed to be a list of rules for everything.

Because I was not comfortable fellowshipping and socializing with the youth in my church, I began to feel that maybe I wasn't "holy" enough for God. I found myself longing to simply live my life as a Christian, without all the legalism. I found myself praying, "God, can't I just be me?" Also, as I got older, there was pressure from the church to fall into the role that God had ordained for me as a woman. I should be looking for a man to marry and settle down and create a family. I rebelled against this pressure with every fiber in my body. At the time, I didn't entirely understand why these expectations made me so angry. I simply found myself not wanting to go to church at all. As I grew into my later teens, my parents also began to question why I didn't have a boyfriend. It wasn't until much later that I realized what was really going on inside me.

Despite my rebellion of the expectations of my church and even the questioning from my parents, I never felt pressure from God to date men or to get married. My relationship with Christ was a loving one. I always felt that He loved me no matter what. I am so thankful that I did not allow the legalism of my home church to flow into my relationship with Christ. For it has been that close and intimate relationship with Him that has given me hope and guidance throughout my adult life.

Rev. Cyd Andrews-Looper

CHAPTER 2

Oh, to Be a Bo Joe!

After graduating from high school in Pickens, SC, I attended Limestone College, a liberal arts school in Gaffney, South Carolina. It was about an hour-and-a-half from my home. My parents thought it would be a good idea for me to stay on campus. So I moved in with my assigned roommate and began college life.

I quickly found this environment was much too wild for me. I had grown up in a conservative home that was safe. I had never taken any illegal drugs and had only drank one beer. The day I turned eighteen, I stopped at a convenience store and purchased a beer, simply because I could legally do it.

At Limestone, there were parties going on all of the time. My roommate stayed drunk and brought guys back to the room for sex. I felt I was living in a pit of degradation. While I did not consider myself a "goody two shoes," I had not been around this kind of environment. And, the freedom and wildness really scared me. I was one of those kids who was affected by the public service announcement that showed an egg and said…"This is your brain"—then it cut to an egg in a frying pan and said, "This is your brain on drugs." Seeing the excesses of alcohol and marijuana was completely out of my comfort zone. I had always been popular in high school and saw that I could also be popular in this setting if I would simply let go and start drinking all the time and having sex with multiple partners. That was really more than I could handle. So after I completed one year, I told my parents I was transferring to Bob Jones University, a fundamentalist school that my home church supported. I think the freedom and excesses that I saw at Limestone College really frightened me. I had grown up in a protective environment with lots of rules. I began thinking that perhaps I needed to give "the rules" another chance. Somehow they felt much safer than the outrageous freedom that I saw the year prior. In the fall of 1982, I moved into the dorm room with three other roommates. This school was the complete opposite of the former school. No alcohol, drugs or cigarettes, no playing cards, dancing, etc. were allowed on or off campus. Girls could not bring guys even into the dormitory lobby. Men and women who wanted to see each other made an appointment for the "dating parlor." This was a large room that looked like a furniture store. I never went there because I had no desire to date any guy. Since high school, I had learned the fine art of keeping guys at a distance. I maintained enough of a masculine look that no guy asked me out. I had a great sense of humor and they loved being my friend. But, I was safe from them having any romantic interest in me.

The first and second semester at Bob Jones, I flourished. Though I had to wear dresses every day, it was a safe environment. I was a speech major and loved my classes. I also met a great friend, Dee, whom I have continued to stay in touch with to this day. Dee was also a speech major, but she had a different attitude from many of the other "Bo Joes," a term used to describe individuals who had grown up in this college community. Dee had attended Bob Jones Academy since first grade. She was well known by professors and staff. In addition, her parents were wealthy individuals who supported the mission of the school. Despite her background, Dee couldn't have been more down to earth. She reached out to me and befriended me. I spent time with her at her parents' home. Her dad sponsored a community women's softball team. Dee was the coach, and I was the star player. The women on the team wore jeans and tennis shoes, not skirts or gauchos. Thanks be to God!

Lol

During my second year at Bob Jones, I began to have conflicts. Every major at the university carried with it a list of expectations that included ability, attitude, and outward appearance; but being a speech major carried a number of expectations regarding dress and poise. I had the ability to communicate well; however, I was too masculine for the professors who were assessing me. At the beginning of the second year, every speech major had to undergo speech trials. This included reciting a poem, performing a play through oral interpretation with characters on the dramatic "V," and giving a speech on a topic about which we were passionate. I scored well on the oral interpretation piece and the speech. My score for the poetry recitation was low, and my scores for poise and dress were below average. This was a difficult moment in my life. One's outward appearance was very important to the Bob Jones community in general; but for speech majors, it was of the utmost importance. There was a part of me that was embarrassed and another part of me that was angry. I was embarrassed that I couldn't be more like Dee, and angry that the professors required me to be more feminine. It wasn't that I was extremely masculine. It was that I simply wasn't feminine enough to be a "proper" speech major. Deb wasn't extremely feminine. She had short hair much like mine and she was a bit overweight. But Dee knew how to carry herself in a dress, and she kept her nails manicured and polished. She also wore five-hundred dollar suits.

The rest of that year was quite difficult for me. I felt like I was being judged too harshly on things that did not matter. I knew I could improve my delivery of poetry, and I knew that I could increase my confidence and soften my outward appearance. However, something inside me began to question why I was at Bob Jones. They had created models of perfection for every major. It wasn't solely about meeting academic standards. Students who could not meet either the academic or other expectations (having the right look, the right clothes and carrying themselves in the right way) of their major were "conditioned." That meant they could continue taking classes in their major; but they would not be given a degree until they met all the expectations fully. There was a part of me that questioned whether I could ever meet the expectations they had for a speech major. I knew I could meet the academic requirements; however, when it came to standards of dress and hair care and nail care and makeup—how they were expecting me to present myself did not align with the person inside of me. So at the end of that school year, I left and never returned.

I went to work in the fall for a local television station, where a friend of mine worked. For the next year, I worked there full time. I wore my jeans and tennis shoes to work and had a big smile on my face! I attended church off and on. I was experiencing a battle within. My experience of my home church followed by what I had gone through at Bob Jones made me feel like I could never live up to the expectations that God had for me as a woman. I remember praying when alone, "God, why can't I just be myself and do what I am comfortable doing?" The only role models I had of Christians were in the fundamentalist faith in which I had grown up. The young women I had gone to Sunday school with were now married and having children. I felt I was growing further and further from God's expectations for my life.

CHAPTER 3

What is a Wesleyan?

The fall of 1984, when I went to work at the television station, my younger sister enrolled at Southern Wesleyan University, a small, Christian, liberal arts school sponsored by the Wesleyan Church. They were conservative and evangelical, but seemed much more practical than Bob Jones in living out their faith. My sister seemed to enjoy SWU very much. Also, the woman I was in love with, Monica, was planning on enrolling at SWU in the fall.

Yes…I was in love, or at least I thought I was at the time. I met this woman at a part time job I had with a local department store while at Bob Jones. (You won't believe it, but I worked in handbags and hosiery!!!! #this is just wrong#) Monica and I both battled guilt and shame due to what we had been taught about two women being together. In general, the relationship was codependent and unhealthy. Nevertheless, Monica convinced me to go talk to the financial aid office. I did and made plans to also enroll the fall of 1985. This was one of the best decisions I could have made, and in retrospect I believe it was part of God's plan for my life.

Over the next three years, I began to grow spiritually in a way I never thought possible. Two things encouraged my growth. First, this school did not have strict standards for dress. I could wear my jeans and tennis shoes to class!

#Hello!# I could also wear them to chapel every day. SWU did not focus on legalistic issues of dress and hair styles but rather on getting an education and growing in your relationship with God. The second thing that encouraged my growth was that I saw women pursuing their call to the ministry.

The Wesleyan Church from its inception has ordained women into ministry. Therefore, the school did not assign strict gender roles to students. They simply encouraged you to follow your dreams and to be obedient in your relationship to God—music to my ears and heart! Their support and acceptance allowed me to remove the walls which I had put up in my relationship with God. For the first time in my life, I felt hopeful that I could actually please God with my life.

In addition to daily chapel services there was a spiritual emphasis week each semester. During this week, the university brought in gifted Christian speakers who knew how to challenge youth for Christ. I began to develop a very personal relationship with Jesus Christ. I was amazed at how much I enjoyed praying and studying Scripture. They didn't address issues related to sexual orientation. They didn't define what I should wear or how I should fix my hair, etc. They focused on where you were in your relationship with God.

For the first time in my life, I felt completely loved and accepted by God. It wasn't about my sexual orientation at the time. It was that I was simply accepted as a woman who did not fit into the expectations of my gender…and that was ok. I served on a summer ministry team. I had many opportunities to share my faith with teenagers. As a camp counselor at a different camp each week, I would be assigned 10-15 teenage girls. I shared devotions with them each night before we went to bed. I sat with them during the evening worship services. I sat with them during meals and would let them talk about whatever was on their minds. I got to know them and I let them get to know me. It was incredibly exciting to see those young people place faith in Christ. God used those moments to build my faith and confidence in Jesus Christ. I learned that I could trust Him not only with my life, but also with the lives of others was well.

I had grown up with fundamentalist Baptist theology, a branch of Calvinism. The Wesleyan Church was Arminian in theology. Both branches are conservative in their faith and interpret scripture literally. The difference is the weight that they give particular verses from which their theology springs. I had heard the term "Arminianism" at Bob Jones; but did not understand what it meant. Students were not allowed to discuss Arminian theology. Bob Jones was strictly Calvinist. Now there are varying degrees of Calvinism. There are the extreme "5-point" Calvinists who believe in the 5 points defined by John Calvin. The acronym is TULIP. This stands for Total depravity (nothing good within the human heart, Unconditional election (God does not base His love on anything He sees within the human heart), Limited Atonement (Christ died only for the elect…that is, those chosen by God to receive salvation), Irresistible grace (when God showers His chosen with His love they cannot resist it), Perseverance of the Saints (if you have received God's love and accepted it…<you really have no choice because it is irresistible>…you cannot lose your salvation…or fall from grace). I soon learned that there were beliefs in the Wesleyan Church that clashed with the Baptist theology of my roots. The biggest was the belief that a person who has accepted Jesus Christ by faith can "fall from grace." My Baptist theology had taught me that once I placed child-like faith in Jesus Christ as God's Son and Savior, my soul was eternally secure.

The Wesleyans told me that if I said a cuss word and died, I would go to hell. The Wesleyans believed that human beings were inherently good and that sin was any conscious act done against God. My salvation through Wesleyan theology was dependent upon me continuing to cooperate with God and do well. If I chose to act in a way that was unkind or participate in behaviors not becoming of a Christian (drinking alcohol, cussing, dancing, etc.), then God released me until I asked for forgiveness. If I sinned and died before having an opportunity to ask forgiveness, I would go to hell. The Baptists believed that we, as human beings, were inherently sinful. We sinned daily because we were fallen spiritually. Our salvation was completely dependent upon the grace of God. It was God who saved us and God who kept us safe spiritually.

The Wesleyan theology of "falling from grace" seemed really extreme to me. I remember my home church referring to this theology as "salvation by works." I had always been taught that salvation is by grace through faith; that it is a gift from God. I had been taught that there was nothing that I could do to earn it other than to simply believe in the work that Christ had done for me on the cross and be eternally grateful for His mercy and grace.

The Wesleyans also believed that salvation was from God. However, they believed we had to cooperate with God in order to receive the salvation. That is, we had to believe and live a holy life in order to receive eternal peace and salvation. Their view of the Baptists' eternal security doctrine was that it allowed individuals to cheapen Christ's work on the cross. If all one had to do was simply believe and "get your fire insurance and then live like the devil," then the Baptist Church was sending many unsuspecting individuals to eternal damnation. I remember having extensive conversations and debates on this issue with fellow students at SWU.

The more I studied and prayed, the more I felt that perhaps the truth was somewhere in the middle. I saw salvation as a gift from God. We receive it by faith in Jesus Christ as Son of God and Savior. But this faith is the beginning of a covenant relationship with God. If we are growing in spiritual knowledge and faith, we will seek to be holy and faithful as we live out that faith. As James says, "Faith without works is dead." I do not believe we are saved because of our works. I do believe our salvation will bring about loving deeds for others and heartfelt worship to God.

The summer following graduation, I traveled once again with a ministry team. This time I was the road manager for the musical group. Basically, I was to make sure we reached each destination safely. I was responsible for paying for food and gas and keeping up with the receipts. I was responsible for making sure the group behaved appropriately as we represented SWU in camps, churches and conferences. It was exciting to see God working in me and through me and the team to reach other people for Christ. Though I never really thought about the ministry in terms of vocation, I knew that I could live out faith in lay ministry and pursue a career in a field of service.

Rev. Cyd Andrews-Looper

CHAPTER 4

God, You Want Me to What?

My call to ministry began in 1991 when I was 29 years old. I was working for the state of South Carolina as a community educator for the local Alcohol and Drug Abuse Center. I had graduated in 1988 with a Bachelor's degree in psychology. I assumed I would work for the state while pursuing a Master's in social work or psychology. While I had always had a concern and felt a connection to those who were lost or hurting, I never envisioned myself in ministry. The reason was partially because I was a woman and had been taught from an early age that God doesn't call women to ministry; and partially because the ministry seemed much too serious for me. God had gifted me with a sense of humor, and all the ministers I had ever seen were very serious and holy.

When I began to sense a calling into ministry, it really frightened me. I assumed that it was the spiritual enemy trying to lead me astray. I kept hearing the verses in the New Testament about women keeping silent in church and not having authority over men. Although by this time, I personally knew women who had followed their call to ministry, I still could not turn off the tape recorder in my head that told me this could never be God's will for me as a woman.

I found myself becoming more and more miserable with my job at the state. It wasn't a bad job. It just wasn't where God really wanted me. I looked in the newspaper every weekend for job opportunities; but there were none. I became very frustrated and felt like God did not care about my unhappiness. My time with God consisted of a quick 15—minute devotion followed by my plea for God to find me another job.

In September of 1991, I was invited to attend a weekend spiritual retreat. I went because I wanted to be with Monica—I was still head over hills in love with her—not because I expected to gain anything spiritually. The relationship that I had with her was very codependent. I would have been completely fine just being "more than friends and less than partners" for the rest of my life. I valued the emotional connection. And, as long as we weren't acting on our desires (having sex), we weren't sinning. Looking back, it was an extremely unhealthy relationship.

I left with Monica on Friday after work. We arrived in the evening in time to register and eat dinner. The next morning, we got up early and ate breakfast. Then we went to the first session. The speaker issued a challenge to everyone in the auditorium: to spend an hour alone with God that day. Well, that seemed like an eternity to me. I was a bit upset with God for not listening to me. But as the speaker continued, the Spirit began to speak to me. I sensed God saying, "Please just listen to him and do it."

When the session was over, I took my Bible and notebook and found a quiet space. I read some of my favorite scripture passages and said a prayer… about ten minutes had passed. I wondered what in the world I was going to do for the next 50 minutes with God. I read through my favorite scripture passages again and then read several Psalms. By this time, 30 minutes had passed. This was just too hard. "What in the world does a person do with an hour with God?" I thought. It had become hard to really focus on God when I felt like I wasn't being heard. I sat staring out the window.

I remember hearing the heating unit come on. I remember hearing the pops and cracks in the room. I closed my eyes and just sat listening. Eventually, I couldn't hear the hum of the heating unit or the pops and cracks. My soul got quiet. And the quieter my soul became, the more I sensed God's presence in the room. I felt such love in that moment. I began to cry. The constant thought in my mind was, "I love you, Cindy." It was God talking to me in my thoughts. I continued to sit quietly with my eyes closed. I continued to "listen" to God speak.

God told me how He had longed to have time with me. God told me that He had desperately wanted to talk to me, but that I had not given Him time to do so. For the longest time, He simply told me how much He loved me. Then He repeatedly asked this question, "Cindy, do you trust Me?" I responded in my thoughts, "Yes, Lord, I do trust You."

Again, the Spirit would say, "Cindy, do you trust Me?" And again, I would say, "God, yes, I do trust You." Then the Spirit began to share with me that He had seen me calling out to Him; that His heart had broken over the little time I had given him. He explained that He knew how unhappy I was in my job and that He had desperately wanted to comfort me. "Today is the first time you have given me time to speak to you," God explained. I have longed to hold you closely and give you my words of hope. "Cindy," God said, "I want you to resign your position at work."

At this point, I opened my eyes quickly and very wide…as I believed the enemy must have arrived. This was outrageous and off the spiritual deep end! Only weird, whacked-out charismatics would listen to something so crazy. I thought about packing my things, but the peace I felt there in God's presence was difficult to leave. So I closed my eyes again and began to quiet my soul once more. And God once again spoke, "Yes, Cindy, it is Me—and, yes, I said I want you to resign your position at work."

There was no way I was going to let this go without an argument. "So, God," I said, "If you want me to resign my position, you could at least give me a date?" And immediately, January 1st, 1992 popped into my mind. By this time, I was expecting to get the gift of speaking in tongues and just become a full-fledged charismatic. I was certainly starting to feel like one!

"So, Lord, let me get this right. You want me to resign my position at work on January 1, even though you haven't gotten me another job yet?"

And God said, "Cindy, do you trust Me?"

I left that weekend retreat confused and heavy in spirit. I knew God had clearly spoken to me. But I also knew that there was no way I could put in my resignation without having another job lined up. My parents had taught me better than that. The next two weeks were very difficult. I couldn't sleep or eat. One of my Christian coworkers stopped me as I was passing by her office. She asked what was wrong. I sat down in her office and blurted out everything that had happened at the retreat. She said, "Well, Cindy, I think you need to be obedient."

"But this is crazy—only people who have dropped off the spiritual deep end do things like this," I said.

She closed her door and said a quick prayer for me. The next day, I wrote my letter of resignation. I could not handle the inner turmoil any longer. Basically, I told God that I felt like a complete idiot to even consider this, and I hoped He wasn't trying to play some kind of mean joke on me. I put the letter in my boss's box and was amazed at the deep sense of peace I felt. I felt God smiling at me, even with my attitude flaring.

CHAPTER 5

God, You Weren't Kidding!

As the weekend came, I once again looked in the paper for possible jobs—and as usual, there were none. Part of me became overwhelmed and frightened, thinking "what in the world have I done!" But another part of me was at peace—peace like I had never known. I once again closed my eyes and listened, and God simply said, "Just trust Me. I do have a plan."

About a month and a half went by, and I still had not even a glimmer of hope for finding a job. By this time, it was late October and deep doubts were setting in. How many employers hire individuals at the end of the year? Not many. But each time I grew anxious, I would close my eyes and listen, and God would always say, "Cindy, just trust Me."

The first week of November I received a call from the Director of Alumni Relations at Southern Wesleyan University. She explained that she was going to be retiring and they were starting to interview candidates to fill the position. She said they had received a number of résumés, but she had been thinking of me the last several days, so she decided to give me a call. I shared with her that I was looking for a job and would send my résumé immediately. The next week, I got a call from the Vice President of Development asking me to come for an interview. Two days later, I was being interviewed by him and the Director of Alumni Relations. The interview went well and I sent a thank you note. The next week, I got another call from the Vice President asking for a second interview. This time it was with the College President and several chairs of departments in addition to the Vice President.

Again, I felt the interview went well; however, I assumed they would want someone a bit older than me. The university donors tended to be older, well-established individuals. In fact, most of them were old enough to be my parents or grandparents. The Vice President of Development walked me to my car after the second interview and said, "Cindy, we are very impressed with you. I'd like to offer the position to you right now. It will actually begin January 1st since the current director be will retiring December 31st."

I teared up and explained to my future boss the journey of faith I had been on since September. He congratulated me on my willingness to step out in faith and asked me to let him know by the next day if I would like to take the position. I assured him that I would and told him that I felt this turn in my career was clearly part of God's plan for my life.

This three-month journey of faith was truly a Godsend for me. I learned in those moments that God cared about me and had a plan for my life. I also learned that I had to make time to listen to the Spirit in order to know the steps I should take.

While I was a student at SWU, the staff, faculty and alumni watched me grow spiritually. They saw me assuming various positions of leadership and leading effectively. When dignitaries came to the university, I was one of the students who was asked to meet them. I knew how to behave and have stimulating conversations. I was seen as a "model student" spiritually and academically. When I applied for the position, I think they saw me as the perfect person to represent the alumni of the university.

January 1, 1992, I began a new chapter in my life. I also began a closer relationship with Jesus Christ. This was truly a turning point in my faith journey. God became more real than ever!

Rev. Cyd Andrews-Looper

CHAPTER 6

A Love Lost

The year 1992 was a critical point in my faith journey. In January, I began a job that God had clearly given me. But, the fall of 1992 brought one of the lowest points of my life. I had been in a hidden relationship with Monica for ten years. I think I clung to her because I thought it was the best I could hope for given my faith background. We had an unhealthy emotional connection and were seldom intimate. When we were intimate, there was a great deal of guilt on her part. Physical intimacy was usually followed by Bible study and prayer in hopes of being forgiven and cleansed from "our sin." I also think this "arrangement" seemed safe given my faith, which opposed two women being romantic partners.

Monica had a beautiful singing voice and we both enjoyed drama. We actually created a ministry together and traveled occasionally; we performed Christian sketches together and Monica sang. We both loved God and wanted to share our faith with others.

In the fall of 1992, while I was traveling for my job, Monica called me and told me she was dating a man. She was in her mid-thirties and wanted children. And, she was tired of dealing with the guilt and shame of this "sinful lifestyle." This news hit me in a deep place. I had come to see our relationship as something that appeared to be accepted within the college and church community. Everyone knew that if I was attending something, she would be there and vice versa. They saw us as single women who were the best of friends. Certainly, some folks may have suspected more. But, in general, we were known as two very funny Christian women who shared a close bond.

In the weeks that followed as I began seeing her out in public with this man, something inside me snapped. She was spending more and more time with him, which left no room for me in her life. No one had known about our feelings for each other, so they didn't entirely understand why I was so upset. And, I couldn't exactly tell them that we had been romantically involved for the last ten years. The pain of this loss combined with having no support as I faced it brought me to a place of hopelessness. This was the first time that I had really looked at myself honestly and admitted that I was indeed…gay. Being in this pseudo-relationship kept me in a safe space spiritually because I wasn't really in a lesbian relationship. I just happened to be emotionally attached to a woman. So, somehow in my mind, it was "ok" before God.

But, with Monica starting to date this man, I had to look at myself alone before God and admit that I was gay. And everything I had been taught about homosexuality was that it was sinful…an "abomination before God." Facing the loss of her presence in my life and having to deal with the shame of being gay brought me to the place where I simply wanted to die. I felt so very alone with all the shame and loss. The emotional and mental pain I experienced daily was excruciating. So, one night, I sat on the edge of my bed. I opened the drawer of the night stand and pulled out a small .22 pistol that I had gotten from my dad. I simply could not bear the emotional and spiritual pain any longer. The hell I was living had to end. I put the gun to my temple and was ready to pull the trigger. In that moment, though I never saw them, my bedroom filled with angels and ministering spirits—the presence of God was so real that the room felt static with energy. In that moment, though I never heard an audible voice, God began speaking to me. I had become well-tuned to God's voice. And, He was speaking loudly and boldly to my spirit. He said, "Cindy, STOP! Do not do this! I have plans for you that you cannot see at the moment. I love you with an eternal and everlasting love. I love you and created you just as you are. You are no mistake. I have plans for you: plans to prosper you and not to harm you. Plans to give you hope and a future. Cindy, please trust Me now as you have trusted Me in the past. This moment does not define the rest of your life. I have amazing plans for you. You will be My mouthpiece, communicating my love and hope to many. Please trust Me." (It was in these moments in which God gave me Jeremiah 29:11, and it has been my life verse ever since.)

I put the gun down, and it was as if God climbed in bed with me and wrapped me up in His love. As I stared into the darkness and held tightly to my Bible, I knew this was one of the moments when God was carrying me because I could not do this alone.

The next morning was Saturday. God told me to take the gun to my parents' house. I carried my Bible with me because it was a physical representation of God's presence. Dee, my friend from Bob Jones, also reached out to me unexpectedly at this time. (I believe this was God prompting her. God knew that I needed support) She had no idea initially what was going on, though I eventually felt safe enough to share everything with her. And, as a true friend, she told me that she was there for me and would walk with me during this difficult time.

Thankfully, Dee lived up to her promise. Monica eventually married the man she was dating. The weekend of the wedding in the fall of 1993, Dee planned a trip out of town and invited me to come along. She kept me busy and helped keep me focused on positive things. To this day, I am thankful for the friendship she offered me in those very difficult moments of my life. I have never felt so much shame and pain and absolute aloneness. God used her to give me the confidence to eventually start using my skills in speaking and acting to start my own ministry.

It was also during this time that God began calling me to ministry again. The difference this time was—I did not hesitate. I went immediately to the chair of the Religion Department and sought guidance on how best to move forward. They were starting a new schedule for their Master's in Ministry program that would allow me to continue working at the university while taking classes. It was an accelerated program with classes every weekend. I graduated in May of 1993 with a Master's in Ministry from Southern Wesleyan University.

I did not know what kind of ministry God would call me to do, but I knew I had taken the appropriate steps of preparation. I also began the path for ordination in the South Carolina district of The Wesleyan Church. It was wonderful to have the leadership in the district affirm my gifts and graces for ministry. I was assigned a mentor in ministry who would counsel and guide me through the process.

In January 1994, I began my own ministry called Reality Check. I combined my gifts of humor and public speaking to form a unique outreach ministry. In addition to the preaching, I also did stand-up comedy and had a list of characters that I used to challenge the listeners to hear God's truth. Reality Check flourished beyond anything I thought possible: I think its success was in large part due to the prominence of humor. I have yet to meet a person who does not like to laugh. And I found out that humor disarms us. It allows individuals to bring down their inner walls long enough to hear God's truth. I traveled almost every weekend ministering to churches, women's conferences, and youth conferences. I assumed that this would be my path in ministry. The District Superintendent of South Carolina was proud of my success and opened as many doors as possible for me to continue growing my ministry.

Rev. Cyd Andrews-Looper

CHAPTER 7

Another Living Nightmare

My travels with Reality Check took me across the United States a number of times. It was not unusual for the District Superintendent to meet with me when I was in Central, SC. I tried to meet with him at least monthly. I had always appreciated his support, guidance and encouragement. So when I received a call from him on Monday morning in November of 1995 asking if we could meet on that Wednesday, I did not think anything of it.

However, when I arrived at his office, the secretary was not there to greet me. He came out of his office along with the Assistant District Superintendent and invited me into the boardroom. My meetings with him usually occurred in his office. He was always cheerful and upbeat; however, this day he didn't smile much and the atmosphere was static. We walked into the boardroom and I sat down. The two men took a seat on each side of me. The District Superintendent began to speak, "Cindy, we have found out some grave and disappointing news about you."

He went on to explain that he had received a call from the minister of the University Church, who was my mentor in ministry. Through a series of unexpected events, he had become aware that his daughter and I were dating. She had gotten very sick and her parents had come to Boone to take her home for two weeks. While her parents were in her apartment, her mother found a card I had given her—the beginning of a living nightmare for me.

Renee and I had been dating for about a year. She was completing her master's degree at Appalachian State University in Boone, North Carolina. We were only able to see each other about every other month because of my travel schedule.

The District Superintendent shared that he and others had "suspected" that I had "homosexual tendencies." The fact that I expressed little or no interest in men at my age was a telltale sign. He explained that he and his assistant had discussed the situation and had come up with several options. The first was for me to go immediately into an ex-gay residential facility. I was to never talk to or see the woman with whom I had developed a relationship. I was to cancel my bookings over the next three months and pursue sexual healing for my "homosexual issue." Following my stay in the ex-gay facility, I would be evaluated and allowed to minister to groups that would not "provide temptation" for me.

So this meant, in their minds, that I would most likely never be allowed to speak at another women's conference. It also meant that I would have to have constant supervision when interacting with youth or single women. In general, the nature and scope of my ministry would be very restricted from that point forward. The District Superintendent, whom I had admired on many levels, sat by me and made me feel like I was possessed by Satan. He explained that my sins were an abomination to God and that if I did not repent immediately, my soul was damned for hell. He went on to share how gravely disappointed he was in my choices. He never thought I would fall into such a state of sin that I would actually act on my "urges." And above all, he was disappointed that I would "target" my mentor's daughter to fulfill my sinful desires. I have never in my life felt so shamed and dirty and abhorrent.

The second option they gave me was to resign my position immediately and leave the ministry altogether. They explained that they would prefer that I remain "under their spiritual care" in these moments. But if I did not think I could "abide by their disciplinary expectations," it would be best for me to leave completely. I told them that I needed some time to pray, and think, and that I would be back in touch with them by the beginning of the following week.

Getting into my car, I was numb both physically and emotionally and in a near state of shock. I had a difficult time remembering my way home. I finally made it home, and I lay in my bed feeling like my very breath was abhorrent to God. The experience with these two men had literally robbed me of my sense of identity in Christ. I had been told that I was no longer in the fold, and I needed to repent of my sins to find my way back.

I held my Bible close to me and was able to cry myself to sleep that afternoon. I slept until early evening when the phone ringing woke me. I answered in a groggy and incoherent voice. On the other end was the woman I loved. She was immediately concerned and asked what was wrong. All I could come out with in that moment was, "They know—they know about us—they don't want me to see or talk to you anymore." She began to cry with me.

"What are we going to do?" she asked. And we continued a lengthy and emotional conversation until we had to hang up because we were sobbing and could not talk any longer. My heart felt like lead weighing down my soul and sharp knife-like pains were shooting through my chest.

"Dear God," I cried out, "why does it have to be this way? Why can't I love this person and have your blessing and the blessing of this church?" I turned over and held my Bible even closer, and in those painful moments I sensed God's presence in the room. It was a presence of peace and love. I felt God put His arms around me as I lay on the bed. I once again cried myself to sleep.

CHAPTER 8

God's Got This

When morning came, my body felt too heavy to move. As the room grew brighter and I awakened more fully, I realized that it wasn't a nightmare I had dreamt, but a nightmare I was living. What was I going to do with my life? How could I ever find peace and recover from all of this shame? Dozens of questions went through my mind. It was dizzying to be awake, and I began to feel nauseous. The Sprite I sipped helped some, but the heaviness and shock would not be calmed. I stayed in bed that entire day. Sometimes I would cry until I had no more tears. Sometimes I would stare into space for what seemed like hours. In the late afternoon, I checked my messages. There were more than a dozen—most from Renee. She was heartbroken as well. But it felt like there was nothing else I could do. The last message was from my mom asking me to come to dinner on Friday night.

I knew I needed to compose myself enough to return her phone call. So I got out of bed and took a shower. Afterward, I called her, and though she had no idea what was going on, she had such comforting words for me. "Cindy, you sound so tired," she said. "I have missed you so much. Why don't you come and spend the night with me and your dad tomorrow night? I'll fix a nice dinner and we can spend some quality time together." That really sounded nice to me. Since I traveled a lot, I seldom ate a home-cooked meal.

"Mom," I said, "I am okay. Just dealing with some things. What would be helpful is if I could just come and be with you and Dad and not feel like I have to answer a lot of questions. Does that make sense?"

"Yes, honey, it does make sense. You have to minister to so many people; I'm sure you're emotionally and physically exhausted. Just come and stay with us and we'll make sure you have some time to relax and renew." Though my mother had no idea about my sexual orientation and our relationship had never been close, the conversation with her was familiar and very comforting. She made me feel loved in those brief moments.

I pulled out a piece of paper and began to write. It was a letter to God. I never lashed out at God in these moments. I simply laid out the current situation and told him that I didn't know what I was supposed to do.

As I wrote the letter, I felt God's presence and I felt God's love for me. Somehow, the shame I had been feeling was lessening and the heaviness was lifting. I played one of my favorite Christian CDs while I wrote my long letter to God. I found myself writing down my life story. I shared honestly about how I had always felt different. I told God that I had never felt an attraction to men. I told God that at a very young age, I loved how I felt when being close to women and how during puberty, my raging hormones were directed at the girls in my class, not the guys.

I explained how difficult it was for me to not fit in during high school. If it had not been for my sense of humor, I am not sure what I would have done. I actually was quite popular, not because I fit in; but because everybody loved my sense of humor. I laid out my entire life to God, and with each sentence

I wrote I felt more love and acceptance. It was as if the Holy Spirit was saying, "Yes, I know that—and that as well—yes, I knew about that, too—and I love you—I did not make a mistake—you are not an abomination to Me—I love you." By the time I finished the letter, which was well into the night, I felt a love and wholeness like I had never experienced. I was able to come before God with my head held high and know that my Creator accepted me right where I was. I cried tears of joy. I began to write another letter to God, praising Him for the love and mercy I was feeling. The more I wrote, the more I felt spiritually uplifted.

I felt like everything was going to be okay. I no longer had the heaviness and the dread throughout my body. God had given me back my joy.

Very late in the evening my phone rang. It was Renee. She sounded so pitiful. "I just needed to hear your voice," she said.

"I understand. It is good to hear your voice as well—you know, you are right," I said.

"Right about what?"

"You are right that I should not let them shame me and condemn me to hell."

"Cindy, I miss you. I just want to be close to you right now."

"I know you do and I want that as well, but I need to figure out what to do. I don't think the Wesleyan Church will ever really allow me to minister again. I think if I jumped through every one of their hoops, they'd still keep my spirit in this shameful box. I'm thinking I need to resign and leave the church."

"Wow, are you sure that's what you should do?" she said.

"Well, no, I am not completely sure, but I can't imagine living under the shame that they have laid on me. I also can't imagine not being in ministry. I am just praying and listening right now. Please help me pray about this. More than anything, I want God's will for my life."

"Why don't we pray right now?" she suggested. And we did. Before hanging up, I told her that I loved her and was trusting God to take care of us both. That night, sleep came quickly and peacefully.

CHAPTER 9

When God Carries You

The next morning, I woke up smiling as the sun shone on my face. Somehow I knew that God was at work. I felt a hope and strength far above and beyond my own. I said a prayer of thanksgiving and got out of bed to take a shower. This nightmare that I was living didn't seem so daunting now. God was carrying me.

As I got my things together to stay overnight with my parents, I decided to go ahead and stay the weekend. I knew my mom would love it, and I thought it would do me good as well. I called Mom a little before noon and let her know that I was on my way. She was thrilled that I was coming early and that I was staying the entire weekend.

When I arrived home, I was met by Mom with a big hug and kiss on the cheek. "I am so glad you are here. I'm cooking your favorite meal for dinner. It is just so good to see your face!" Honestly, I've never been that close to my mother. But her words and presence were comforting, though she had no idea what her love meant to me at the time. The weekend was everything I had hoped it would be. God was using my family to minister to me.

On Saturday, my sister Susan, who lived in Nashville with her boyfriend at the time, called me. It had been difficult for my parents when Susan divorced her husband. But the more they learned about him, the more they realized that she had been living with a great deal of verbal and emotional abuse. They desperately wanted her to move back to South Carolina, but she loved Nashville. They also had an issue with Susan living with her boyfriend. These two conservative Baptist parents loved their daughter, but they did not condone her "sinful choices." My thought every time they talked about it was if they only knew about my "sinful choices." My sister invited me to come to Nashville and stay several weeks. My travel schedule during the holidays was always slow, so I decided to go visit her for a couple of weeks in December.

I had about a week in South Carolina before flying to Nashville for a two-week stay with my sister. Before my trip, I sat down to write my letter of resignation to the District Superintendent. I was amazed at how freely the words came. The guilt and shame were all but gone when I put the stamped envelope in the mailbox. There was a tinge of sadness too, though. This decision meant that I was giving up all the dreams I had for building Reality Check into a strong, national ministry. This letter of resignation proved to be a turning point in my life.

Because I wasn't entirely comfortable staying with Susan's boyfriend—he was a nice guy, I just didn't know him and felt weird staying at his house—I chose to get a hotel room not far from where they lived. This ended up being a good idea because it allowed me to have some solitude when I needed it.

While in Nashville, I also did something that I had never had the nerve to do: I called the pastor of the local Metropolitan Community Church (MCC). I had heard about this church but had always been a little frightened to go to one. My perception of "gay people" had been affected by what I had seen and heard in the media. I was not promiscuous and was concerned about a church full of "gay people." The term "gay Christian" sounded like an oxymoron to me; and my conservative roots would not allow me to expose myself to something that seemed theologically liberal. I left a message on the church's answering machine and received a call back in a matter of hours. The pastor's name was Dr. Rembert (Buddy) Truluck, a former Southern Baptist preacher and professor. I could not have talked with someone who understood my hurt more than this man. He shared with me that he had been kicked out of the Baptist College of Charleston and defrocked. Not only did he lose his professional and ministerial standing, he also lost his family. His wife immediately filed for divorce and declared that she would not allow him to see his children, who were in grade school. He did not see his children again until they were young adults.

Dr. Truluck had such a gentle spirit, and he spoke intimately about his relationship with Jesus Christ. I shared my story with him and told him I was trying to find my way from this point forward. "I don't feel condemned by God," I said, "but I find it difficult to reconcile the Scripture passages that seem to clearly condemn homosexual activity."

Before praying with me, he invited me to meet him for lunch and I agreed. While I felt a low level of apprehension about meeting him, I sensed that this was a man who wholeheartedly loved Jesus Christ. So I met him at a local sandwich shop. A man in his late fifties, he had white hair, a magnetic smile, and kind eyes that looked larger than normal through his gold-rimmed glasses. He extended his hand and introduced himself. He had brought his Bible and a file of material.

I ended up spending almost three hours with this generous man of faith. I apologized for taking so much of his time, but he assured me that a large part of the joy in his life came from sharing hope with other LGBTQ individuals who were struggling spiritually. He invited me to come back to Nashville over the New Year to join his church—a small congregation of about 70—in their New Year's celebration. I told him I would do my best to make the effort to return.

He also invited me to the church's upcoming midweek Bible study, which he led in his home. I attended that and for the first time in my life sat by people who also said they were gay and Christian. A warmth and hope filled the room as we all stood and held hands and Dr. Truluck closed the session in prayer.

CHAPTER 10

Reconciliation Is a Process, Not an Event

Back in my hotel room, I poured over all the materials Dr. Truluck had given me in our first meeting. I stayed up well into the early morning hours reading everything in great detail. Much of it seemed foreign to me. The translations of Scriptures were nowhere near what I had been taught in the church I'd grown up in or in my ministry training. I called Dr. Truluck the next day thinking that perhaps I was being led astray with all this "liberal theology." I had a list of questions to ask him. One of the first things I questioned was: Did he really think Ruth and Naomi were lesbian lovers? He explained that some liberal scholars believed that they were two women in love. I told him that if I embraced that as truth, I could never reconcile my faith and the Scriptures that condemn homosexual behavior.

He asked me how I had reconciled the Scriptures concerning women keeping silent in church and not teaching men. I explained that I had sat down with one of the professors of religion who helped me understand that Paul's restrictions had to do with the fact that women at the time had no religious training; therefore, women were not qualified to teach men. And that it wasn't until the New Testament Church that women could come into the place of worship. This new environment and experience brought many questions for the women. Thus, they were "disruptive" because they sought answers by talking to each other and asking questions of their husbands and fathers.

Neither of these realities were present in the church today; therefore, these restrictions did not apply to the Christian Church today.

Dr. Truluck went on to explain that the same method of interpretation I used to conclude that God did call women to ministry could be used in reconciling my faith and Scripture. He helped me understand that I had been taught, for the most part, a literal interpretation of Scripture. But that I also was familiar with the historical-critical method of interpretation, which would ultimately lead me to the truth I was seeking. I had already used this method when I reconciled my call to ministry as a woman and scripture passages that seemed to say that women should not speak in church. He also gave me the name of Dr. Ralph Blair, president of Evangelicals Concerned, an affirming ministry for gays and lesbians that brings a more conservative angle to some issues.

Two things that Dr. Truluck told me that have stuck with me over the years: first, hold on to Jesus Christ; He will keep your heart and lead you to peace. And second, reconciling faith and sexual orientation is a process, not an event.

Dr. Truluck once again prayed with me and asked the Spirit to reveal truth to me. He asked Christ to hold me and keep me on this journey. I left Nashville hopeful, yet a bit apprehensive as well. I called Renee and asked her if she would like to join me in Nashville over New Year's. She said she would be delighted. And so we made plans to make the drive.

CHAPTER 11

Seeing the Faithfulness of God Once Again

By this time, the S.C. District Superintendent of the Wesleyan Church had received my letter of resignation. He called and left a message begging me to reconsider my decision. He feared the eternal damnation of my soul. He asked that I please contact him.

I knew when I mailed the letter of resignation that I was leaving behind a chapter in my life that I could never visit again. So I never responded to his calls.

The District Superintendent made the minister of the University Church aware of my decision. I had great respect for this man, but there was no way I would ever meet his expectations for my life. I had to let go of my ministerial standing and the relationship I had built with this man in spiritual leadership over me. I sent him a letter of apology and explained that though I had resigned from ministry in the Wesleyan Church, I was still walking closely with Jesus Christ. What complicated that relationship even more was his daughter was the woman I was dating. I had to put him and all the others in the Wesleyan Church in God's hands. While I knew that their concern for me was genuine, I also knew that they had no idea what they were expecting of me and others like me. They were expecting us to live a celibate life. Celibacy, I believe, is a spiritual gift. Those who have received it live it out with light and joy. However, most human beings don't possess it. Physical and emotional intimacy is very much a part of being human. It is a natural, normal and healthy expression of love. To have celibacy mandated is spiritually punitive. It brings spiritual and emotional shame that takes years to get over.

Renee (my girlfriend) and I celebrated New Year's 1996 in Nashville, Tennessee. We met some wonderful people during the four days of our visit. Two women from the MCC, an older lesbian couple reached out to us with such love. They lived in Murfreesboro and when they heard my story they invited me to come live with them for a while. I thanked them for their offer and told them I would definitely think about it and pray about it. They believed that opportunities for starting over would be much greater in Nashville than in South Carolina. While I speculated that they were correct, I wasn't entirely ready to leave South Carolina. I had built relationships in the Wesleyan Church and at Southern Wesleyan. It pained me deeply to lose them.

When I got back to South Carolina, I looked at all the dates I had to cancel for 1996 and it was very discouraging. I had worked so hard to build up my ministry and my schedule was booked well into the summer months. I sat down and began writing the letters of cancellation. It was one of the most difficult things I've ever done. I basically shared that due to circumstances beyond my control, I needed to cancel the scheduled speaking events. It didn't take long for word to get out that I had been "caught in homosexual behavior and was asked to resign from the Church." At the end of the week, I realized that I had no idea what I was going to do in the New Year or with the rest of my life for that matter. I sat in silence and waited on God. Over and over again the faces of these two women from Nashville popped into my mind. I finally got the message and gave them a call. The second week of January 1996, I packed up all my belongings and drove to Murfreesboro, Tennessee. I was received with open arms. That night at the dinner table, Debra and Gail prayed for God to open doors for me to find a job so I could build a new life in Nashville. On the following Monday morning, I started making the rounds of the temporary agencies.

Within a week, I had a temporary job working for the Muscular Dystrophy Association in downtown Nashville. I was thankful for this job, though it wasn't my dream job, for sure. I let every person I met know that I was new in town and I was looking for a permanent job. Because of my bills and desire to move into Nashville, I needed a job that paid at least $25,000. Folks in Nashville were so nice. It felt good to be there and also to be closer to Susan. She was the only family member who knew about my sexual orientation. It felt good to have a family member love and accept me for who I was.

My sister had made contact with a friend of hers whom she had lived with after her divorce. This woman was in her mid-50s and had a large home. She had divorced several years back and rented out rooms to bring in a little extra money. She told Susan that she would rent me a room for $160 a month. I made plans to move the following month. Debra and Gail were two of the dearest individuals. They loved me and supported each of my new steps in life. And when I moved from Murfreesboro to Nashville, they said a prayer for me and asked me to stay in touch.

I had started attending the local MCC after moving to Tennessee. While I wasn't entirely comfortable with everything about the church, I appreciated and respected the ministry of Dr. Truluck. Because the church did not have its own building, it met in the Unitarian Universalist Church on Sunday nights. One Sunday evening, a bit before worship, one of the women from Sunday school class came up to me and said, "I told my boss about you and he said that you need to contact A. K. (I am using initials for anonymity), a local owner of a PR firm." So the next morning, I called A. K.'s office and left a message. She called me back that afternoon and invited me to meet her for coffee in the morning. I showed up in my best suit with résumé in hand. She looked over my résumé and told me she was currently working on a job description for a job that I would be qualified for. She served on the board of the local Senior Citizens Incorporated (SCI) and had been asked to create a job description for a new position: Marketing Director. We had a good chat and she took my résumé to pass along to the Executive Director of Senior Citizens Incorporated.

I received a call from SCI within a week asking me to come for an interview. I knew because I had no professional network in Nashville that I would be at a disadvantage. So I did my homework well for this interview. I visited every senior center in Nashville before the first interview. I spoke with each director and had a good idea of what the marketing needs were from their standpoint. The folks interviewing me seemed very impressed that I would take the initiative to visit so many centers and research Nashville's senior population. I was soon called back for a second interview. It went well, but I wasn't the only candidate they were interviewing. I was told in the second interview that they were considering two others, both of whom had experience and knowledge of the marketing within the Nashville community. I knew from the beginning that being a newcomer to the area would be my greatest weakness. I tried to put a positive spin on being new to Nashville by pointing out that as new blood I could bring a fresh perspective to their organization and to the community at large.

The second interview was on a Monday, and I was told that they would contact me by the following Friday with their decision. I prayed a great deal about this position. I had come to Nashville with a few hundred dollars and was working a temp job that only paid $7 an hour. I knew in order to make it, I needed a professional job such as this one. Friday passed and I heard nothing. By the following Wednesday, I had pretty much given up hope of getting the job.

I was running out of money, and I was getting frightened that I could not make it in Nashville. I remember lying on the bed with my Bible in my hand crying myself to sleep. I felt very alone. Thursday and Friday passed and still I heard nothing about this position. I resigned myself to the reality of working for the temp agency. I went to bed very discouraged that evening.

On Saturday, I woke to my phone ringing. It was Renee calling from Boone, North Carolina, to see if I had heard anything about the job. I told her that I had not and was trying to face the prospect of starting over and preparing to search for other jobs. We talked for about a half hour, and I wished her well as she studied over the weekend. When I hung up, my phone indicated I had a new voice message.

I dialed the number to check messages and could not believe my ears, "Cindy, this is Marion Aaron from SCI. I just wanted to congratulate you on being our choice for this new position. It is around 6:00 p.m. on Friday. Just plan to give me a call on Monday, and I'll let you know what we need to do next. Have a great weekend!"

I almost broke my foot as I bound out of bed and called my girlfriend, Renee, back. She answered on the second ring, and I blurted out, "I got the job! I got the job!" We both were thrilled that a door had been opened. We were making plans for her to move to Nashville after she graduated in May. It would be important for one of us to have a full-time, decent—paying job in order to get an apartment. After I got off the phone with her,

I bowed at the side of my bed and prayed a prayer of thanksgiving to God for taking care of me.

CHAPTER 12

The Pain of Church Politics

When I went to church on Sunday, I had a wonderful praise to share with everyone. I sang the hymn of praise that night with all my heart—truly God was keeping watch over me in a way only the Spirit can. I noticed after the service that several folks were being rather "cliquey," and they seemed to be gossiping about Dr. Truluck. As soon as I approached, they stopped talking. I wasn't sure what was going on, but it didn't feel motivated by Christian love.

Two weeks later, Dr. Truluck left for a three-week trip to South Carolina to care for his ailing mother. During that time, the assistant minister, a woman whom I had never felt very good about, assumed the duties of preaching. I did enjoy her sermons, but after the service she surrounded herself with "the clique." And they would gossip about Dr. Truluck—again, they changed the subject when I sat down. I did not know what they were saying, but I did not like the divisiveness that was apparent. I asked one of the guys who was a good friend of Dr. Truluck what was going on. He told me that there was a group in the church that did not like Dr. Truluck and they were trying to get rid of him. I asked why they didn't like him and the reason given was that he was "too Baptist" in his preaching and leadership. My blood boiled that these individuals, led by the assistant pastor and a Board member, would try to get rid of Dr. Truluck while he was out of town. This seemed anything but Christian to me.

It was during this time that I became aware of the MCC governmental structure. The "Board" was the governing body that made all the decisions for the church. The Board had four individuals on it and a three-fourths majority vote could remove Dr. Truluck from the pulpit. A week later, during a service, the assistant minister made the announcement that Dr. Truluck had resigned as minister of the church. I felt sick to my stomach and got up and left the service.

Later, I learned that three of the board members, which made a quorum, had met and voted Dr. Truluck out of the pulpit while he was out of town caring for his sick mother. The board chair called him in South Carolina to inform him of their decision. This experience really disillusioned me with gay Christians and the MCC. It seemed ridiculous to me that three individuals on a board could vote to remove a minister without it going to the congregation for a second vote. I had never been a part of a church with this style of governance; and I knew from this incident I never wanted to be part of a church that was governed in such a manner.

CHAPTER 13

Dear God, What Are You Doing?

In late February 1996, I began attending a local Methodist Church. I liked the minister and enjoyed his sermons very much. I got to know the assistant minister, and we shared our common call to ministry. She invited me to a prayer retreat at a Penuel Ridge Retreat Center, about an hour outside of Nashville. It was a wonderful day of solitude with God. It was around April by this time. I had started my new job in March and found myself very hopeful.

When I looked back at the beginning of the year, I was amazed at how God had taken care of me. I was looking forward to Renee moving to Nashville the end of May. I began checking around for apartments across Nashville. I liked the Bellevue area very much and decided on an apartment in that area.

The end of May, I rented a U-Haul and drove to Boone, North Carolina. It was so exciting to have Renee moving to Nashville. At the age of 33, for the first time in my life, I was finally going to enjoy a normal family life with a partner. Renee's parents were not happy about her moving in with me, but they knew she was an adult who had the right to make her own decisions; although this did not stop her mother from sending cards reminding her that she was going to hell. She handled her parents' response well. She let them know that conversations about her "going to hell" were off the table. If they brought this topic up, she would end the call and say goodbye. She set good boundaries with them. Her strong faith and confidence as a child of God allowed her to live that out before her parents. They agreed to disagree on this issue. But, she made it clear where the boundaries were and expected them to respect her life and family.

In July, I decided to start a Bible study on Sunday evenings. A good friend, Kevin Boyd, who lived in East Nashville, offered his large living room with 3 loudly colored sofas from the Salvation Army and GoodWill in which to hold the study!! The local MCC had dwindled to less than twenty members. A number of the folks had contacted me wanting to get together. There was an obvious need for spiritual fellowship. I, too, felt the need to study and fellowship with individuals who were like me.

The first night, we had twenty individuals show up for the Bible study. The next week, there were twenty-five. By the middle of August, the number had grown to over forty. We were packed in my friend's living room like sardines. But, there was something wonderfully intimate about it. Folks began to jokingly toss out the idea of starting a church. And I would jokingly tell them that I didn't think that was a good idea. I had no interest in repeating what had happened at the MCC. At the end of August, we had nearly fifty attending the Bible study. It felt good to see an interest in studying God's word. One night after Bible study, Kevin, the young, former Pentecostal man who offered his living room for the study, sat me down and articulated the spiritual needs of the gay community in Nashville.

He ended by telling me that he thought we should start a church from the group attending the Bible study. I shared with him my serious reservations about repeating what had happened at MCC. He responded by telling me about an independent church in Memphis that was predominantly gay and lesbian. He asked if I would make a trip with him to visit the church and talk to the minister. If he made the calls and got everything set up, I told him I would think about it. After I agreed to make the trip, I found out he had already been in contact with the minister about us visiting. It was one of the best things that could have happened.

The Reverend Timothy Meadows pastored Holy Trinity Community Church, the largest predominantly gay and lesbian church in Memphis...and I believe the largest predominately LGBTQ church at that time (early fall 1996). In his earlier career, he had pastored in the Methodist and Episcopal Churches. He, too, had a story of pain and rejection. But he also had a story of reconciliation. He had seen firsthand the spiritual and emotional wounds within the gay community. He explained that Holy Trinity was independent because the local MCC was full of drama and divisiveness. I told him of my experience in Nashville. He said that while there was drama in his church, the leadership structure allowed for all major decisions to be made by the congregation.

I told Tim (the pastor) about our Sunday evening Bible study and how it had grown and flourished. He encouraged me to move forward in starting an independent Christian Church. I was so impressed with Tim and this amazing congregation. I asked him if Holy Trinity of Memphis would receive my ordination. He said he would look over my educational documents and ministry experience and let me know. The worship service at Holy Trinity Memphis was wonderful. There were 150 plus in attendance. They encouraged and congratulated us on the work that was happening in Nashville. We left that weekend hopeful of what could happen in Nashville.

Tim and the church leadership allowed us to use their tax I.D. number as a mission church of theirs until we could get everything in place in Nashville. They came alongside us like loving parents. It was a wonderful relationship that we forged in those first 6-8 months. Because of the relationship we had built and the way this congregation had helped us, we decided to also call our church in Nashville, Holy Trinity Community Church.

When I followed my call into ministry in my twenties, I never envisioned myself in a parish ministry. I saw myself doing what I had done with Reality Check: traveling and speaking. Assuming the leadership and ministry of a local church was daunting to me. But as I prayed, God reminded me to simply trust the Spirit. By this time, God had proven to me many times over that the Spirit was faithful and trustworthy. In the midst of my apprehension, I knew I could trust my relationship with Christ.

We had our first service as a church the beginning of October. We began meeting at the new Senior Citizens Center in Madison. I knew the director and told her I was starting a small church. We paid them $40 a week to meet there on Sunday nights. The local LGBT newspaper sought me out for interviews. The publicity added to our growth quickly. And then the unexpected happened—a reporter from The Tennessean began calling me—day and night—wanting an interview.

CHAPTER 14

I Did Not Sign Up for This!

These calls frightened me terribly. I was not "out" at work and was only "out" to one family member. I had no desire to have my name and story splashed on the front page of the local paper. The reporter was insistent that I meet for an interview. He finally told me that if I did not agree to an interview he would show up after one of our services with a photographer. How unfair to our congregation, I thought. These innocent, hurting people attended our church in search of peace. So I finally agreed to an interview.

We set the interview for a Thursday afternoon at a local coffee shop. The photographer was setting up his lighting when I arrived. The reporter sat down beside me and began asking questions. When the interview was finished, he told me that he thought the story would run in either Sunday's or Monday's edition.

I awoke the next morning to my phone ringing at 7:00. It was a local radio station wanting to talk to me. My blood went cold. While I got in the shower, my partner went out to get a copy of the paper. My thoughts raced and anxiety rushed over me—much like the feeling I had the day I drove away from the office of the District Superintendent.

This time, however, I didn't feel condemned, just fearful of the backlash from my employer and others who knew me. As I got dressed for work, the phone continued to ring. It was radio stations and several TV stations. This was getting out of hand, and I did not know what to do. I stopped answering the phone. On my way to work, I had this dread in my soul. I was going to have to face my boss, and I fully expected her to say, "You're fired!"

As I drove down West End, I remember praying, "Dear God, please help me—I am afraid—I never expected to be facing this—I need your help and strength in these moments." The Spirit, as always, simply said, "Cindy, just trust me. I love you and I will take care of you." Knowing that God was going before me in this journey made it easier.

When I walked into the Senior Citizens Center on Division Street that day, I felt like everyone was staring at me. I went directly to my office and shut the door. Several of my colleagues who knew about my sexual orientation came to my door and knocked. They were concerned about how I was doing.

They told me the Director of the Center had taken the paper out of the lobby as soon as she saw the article. The seniors were wondering who stole the morning paper! My colleagues assured me that they were supporting me in all this. Their words were comforting. It wasn't long before I got the expected call from my boss, the Executive Director. She asked me to come to her office. I climbed the stairs just knowing that when I came back down, I would be without a job.

I reluctantly walked into her office—feeling like a sheep going to slaughter. I made brief eye contact with her. She did not smile. She began by saying, "I assume you know why I have called you to my office." I nodded my head affirmatively. She then proceeded to ask me why I had agreed to an interview with

The Tennessean. "Because the reporter threatened to show up after one of our services with a camera," I said.

"Cindy, why in the world didn't you share that with me? The editor of The Tennessean is a personal friend. I would have gotten the reporter off of you," she said kindly.

"Janet, there was no way I could come to you and say, 'Hey, I'm a lesbian and I've started this church and a reporter at The Tennessean is all but stalking me. Can you help me?'"

"You were afraid to come to me?" she asked.

"Well, yes. I've never come out at work before, and I assumed that you would fire me if you knew; just as I assume you are going to fire me now."

"Cindy, I am not going to fire you," she said. "But we are going to have to figure out how to handle this situation. You all are meeting in our newest Senior Center in Madison, which will have its grand opening next month. This story creates some major PR issues for us. I personally have nothing against you or your church. I am a liberal Methodist myself, but the seniors in Madison will not handle this news well at all," she said.

"Just tell me what you need me to do," I said.

"Well, if you can find another meeting place by the end of the month, I think that would be helpful. If I can assure the seniors at Madison and the state representative who is from Madison that your church is no longer using the facility, I believe we will be fine."

I assured her that I would find another meeting place for the church right away. The issue was never brought up again by my boss, though I felt judgmental undertones from some of my colleagues. One woman blatantly told me that I was a false prophet!

I was able to get another meeting space for the church at a local Unity Church. We continued to meet on Sunday evenings. This space worked well for our needs at the time.

Rev. Cyd Andrews-Looper

In January of 1997, my partner and I bought a two—bedroom condo. This was cause for celebration for both of us. We now owned our own home and could settle down as a couple.

I chose not to renew my contract in July of 1997 with SCI. I felt like I had accomplished all that I could for the organization in the eleven months I worked for them. I had partnered with the development department to create a new program that brought in a regular stream of new income. I also built a relationship with a man who eventually gave over $100,000 to the organization. I decided to concentrate on my work at Holy Trinity and to get a part—time job to supplement my income. My hope was that the church would eventually grow enough to support me full time and that the extra hours and effort I was putting into the congregation would help in growing the church.

CHAPTER 15

The Joy of Parenthood & Pain of a Breakup

During this time of career transition, Renee and I decided to have a baby. We went through the process of artificial insemination, and she became pregnant on the first try. She was expecting in July, 1998. We both had our last names legally hyphenated so that the baby would have both our last names. At this time in Tennessee, this was the only option for a second parent to have any legal ties to a child. In the absence of a father, the child is automatically born with the last name of the mother. My last name became Andrews-Looper and remains so today. Because we have the same last name, I have never been questioned about the validity of my being a parent.

We were so excited about being pregnant. I was glad she was the one carrying the baby. I had never had any interest in "having a baby" though being a parent had always interested me. In the midst of our excitement, neither of us told our parents. We knew the response would not be positive. We couldn't gauge how negative it would be and simply chose to put it off until it was inevitable. Our friends were "over the moon" happy for us and we enjoyed their love and support as we gave updates each month. Hearing our baby's heartbeat for the first time was absolutely amazing!!! It's like the room filled with electric energy as that little heart pounded. When Renee had her first ultrasound and we found out that we were having a little boy…again, it was amazing!! I was hoping for a boy…and statistically, most lesbian couples have boys. The male sperm swim slower than the female sperm and have a longer life. This means the male sperm that are inseminated are more likely to be alive if the egg is released several hours after the insemination.

We started thinking of which boy names we liked right away. Renee had a professor at Appalachian State of whom she was very fond. This professor gave birth to a son during Renee's last year. She named her son "Forrest." Renee really liked that name and I did as well. We just needed to come up with a middle name. I bought a book of baby names and began writing down the ones that I liked. One that I especially liked was "Hayden." When I told Renee, she really liked the name as well. We decided our son's name would be Forrest Hayden Andrews-Looper! That is quite a mouthful! But, we were pleased that we had agreed on a name.

The problem came when he was born and it was time to decide what we were going to actually call him. I'm not sure why we didn't think of this before he was born. But, it wasn't until the day after he was born that it hit us that the movie, "Forrest Gump" had come out a few years before. We feared if we called our child Forrest that everyone would always be saying, "Run, Forrest, run!" *Lol* We decided growing up with two moms would be enough of a challenge. So, we called our beautiful son, Hayden!

In April of 1998, I received a call from Nashville CARES, the local agency that services individuals who are HIV positive. They were looking for a qualified candidate to coordinate their CARE team program and provide pastoral care to their clients. I went for a first and then a second interview and was offered the job in May. I truly believe that God provided that job at just the right moment. Our son was born July 21, 1998. My full-time job at Nashville CARES allowed us to have enough income so that Renee could stay at home with the baby for several months.

Our son, Forrest Hayden Andrews-Looper, was the most beautiful baby I have ever seen. From the first time I held him in the hospital, he took my heart and has never let go. My love for this child grows with each new milestone and experience. Today, he is a handsome, blue-eyed, sixteen-year-old young man. He is truly my pride and joy. Hayden is very intelligent, has a huge heart, and is appreciative of the diversity God created in the world. I believe he will impact the world in some amazing ways!

Renee went back to work full time when Hayden was ten months old. She took a position at Nashville CARES. Obviously, there are positives and negatives of spouses having the same employer. The combination of working in the same office along with our ten year age difference put more stress on the relationship than it could stand. When Hayden was two-and-a-half years old, I moved out of the condo and got my own place. The relationship that I had hoped would last a lifetime was over.

I am choosing not to go into detail concerning all the reasons for the breakup. I honestly see no value in rehashing them. Suffice it to say that breakups are never easy. And, when a child is involved, it is even more complicated. Fortunately, Renee agreed for us to co-parent Hayden. And, eventually, we were able to get legal documents naming me as a co-parent.

The effects that the breakup had on Hayden were he became very clingy. He would not sleep in his own bed and instead of a "blankie," he had a particular kind of pacifier that he wanted in his mouth almost all the time. I would buy 6-7 of these pacifiers at a time. I made the mistake one time of getting the wrong one and regretted it. If it wasn't the one he liked, he would pull it out of his mouth and throw it across the room. And, then he would cry until he got the pacifier he wanted.

The months that followed were some of the darkest in my life. One of the hardest things to deal with was living in the "fishbowl" of the church. Everyone was watching everything that I did and said. I had no place of refuge. I had very few people I could trust with my hurt and feelings. There were harsh judgments laid on me for not staying in the relationship. There were lies and partial truths that were communicated. This created waves of drama that were overwhelming.

Two very dear friends in those moments were Steve Deasy and Phillip Haynes. Steve was the Vestry Chair for the church. The Vestry was the governing body. He was one person who had always supported me. And, he and Phillip were two individuals with whom I felt safe. These guys loved me and reached out to me when I couldn't reach out myself. I remember Valentine's Day coming and waking up with a horrible ache within my heart. After work, I drive to my apartment. Steve & Phillip called and asked if they could come over. I told them, "Sure, I'd love for you to come over." They arrived with a bouquet of roses, a card and chocolate! They said, "We knew today would be difficult for you. We wanted you to know that we love you and are here if you need us." They will never know what that loving gesture meant to me that day. It gave me hope that these difficult moments did not define my future…and it reminded me that I was not alone. They are two of my closest friends today. I also turned to my relationship with Christ, as I had many times before. And while I did go to a counselor who gave me a safe place to process this horrible breakup, ultimately, much of my healing came in my moments alone with God.

CHAPTER 16

A Partner in Ministry

About six months after our breakup, I got up the courage to go out on a date. I had been in a relationship for six and a half years and never envisioned myself dating again. But here I was going through this very intimidating process. I invested a lot of time in working out and eating healthy, which helped my outlook and made a difference in my physical fitness as well. The rest of 2001 was difficult. I remember driving to South Carolina to see my parents over the holidays. I cried most, if not all, the way back because I couldn't stop thinking about how just the previous year I had made the trip with my ex-partner and our son. The loss of my family hurt so badly. I was glad when December 31 was over and January 1 was upon me. My hope was that the New Year would bring continued healing for me.

I dated two women, briefly, during the second half of 2001. But, in 2002, I decided that I needed to just focus on healing emotionally and spend more time alone with God. I put all thoughts of dating out of my mind. I continued my regimen of working out at the gym, spending time with my four-year-old son, making new friends, and restoring my sense of inner peace through my relationship with Christ.

A group of friends who I had gotten to know in 2001 became a bright spot for me in 2002. We would go to movies, play cards, and even play golf on occasion. One individual in particular, Leigh A., caught my attention. She was a tall, beautiful, and poised woman near my age. Her background was similar to mine. Her father and brother were Southern Baptist ministers. She, too, had grown up with conservative roots. I was struck from the beginning by her tender heart and intelligence. She had very strong views on social and political issues, but she was equally passionate about her faith in Christ. I found her attractive on many levels. I could talk so freely about my own faith and experience with her. I enjoyed her company.

We began hanging out together as friends. She traveled a great deal with her job, but when she was in town, we would go see a movie at the local art house theater, just go to dinner, or sometimes order take-out Chinese and watch movies at home. I found myself really loving her company. And one night, coming out of the movie theater, I asked, "So when are you going to fix me dinner?" She gave me a deer-in-the-headlights look that made me want to kick myself for what I'd said. She stuttered a little and said she didn't have much time to cook, but she would love to take me to dinner sometime.

The next day, she sent me an e-mail about the comment I had tossed out. She apologized for how she had handled it and said she would think about "fixing dinner" as a "date." She had assumed that I had no interest in dating her. She went on to say that she would love to take me to dinner or even order dinner in at her place sometime, but that she would consider it a date. I quickly responded back that, yes, indeed, I would also consider it a date and would be delighted to go on a date with her. She looked at her travel schedule, and we made plans to just order in at her home. March 11, 2002 was our first date.

I believe God put this woman in my life for two reasons. One, to help me parent my son. (She has been a wonderful parental figure in his life and her parents have embraced him as a grandson); and two, to contribute her skills in the building of the church God had called me to pastor. Leigh has strong organizational skills, and she can see the big picture as well as the finer details. She understands what pieces are needed to complete the puzzle and how the pieces fit together. Her presence in the ministry of the church since 2008 has been evident—from building the small group ministry to leading and organizing the two-million-dollar capital campaign and managing the build that followed. I was blessed to have her in my life and ministry.

Rev. Cyd Andrews-Looper

CHAPTER 17

Another Step of Faith

The summer of 2004 brought inner turmoil surrounding my job at Nashville CARES. I had been working there since 1998. I had sat by the bedside of over one hundred and sixty individuals who had died. God gave me the greatest honor of walking alongside them in their last days on this earth. God gave me words of comfort to extend to them in their dying moments. God also gave me empathy for the families left behind. I never went to work and felt like I wasn't making a difference in someone's life. God clearly put me in this job; however by 2004, I found myself feeling very burned out, and it was beginning to affect my care and empathy. As I prayed about it, I sensed God calling me to take another significant step of faith.

Again, just as in years past, when I was quiet and listened to the Spirit, I felt called to resign my job. "What am I supposed to do, Lord?" I asked. And clear as day, God said, "I want you to work full time at Holy Trinity." This frightened me as much as, if not more than, the other Grand Canyon moments in my life. I had lived long enough at that point to know I could trust God to take care of me, but the Spirit was calling me to trust God to use the congregation, a group of people that weren't always mature in their faith, to take care of me. I prayed for three months before the inner turmoil was more than I could take.

Finally in November of 2004, I shared what was on my heart with the congregation. It was a very vulnerable moment for me. I simply had to trust that God would place a desire within them to hear the Spirit's words of truth. I had to trust God to open their eyes and hearts to see what the Spirit wanted to accomplish within our congregation.

The response was overwhelmingly positive. The Vestry members, lay ministers, and others in the congregation stepped forward and stood alongside me. We, together as a family of faith, were going to make this journey of faith across the Grand Canyon.

I went to work at Nashville CARES that Monday and submitted my letter of resignation, effective mid-January. I knew the agency would need my input on the year-end reports for my program, so I committed to completing the reports before I left.

On January 16, 2005, I stepped out on faith as the full-time minister of Holy Trinity Community Church. I was so excited to see the congregation stepping alongside me in this journey. We began an active lay ministry program that provided training and accountability. We had congregational meetings at the end of each quarter, and the Vestry recommended budget increases for my salary at each of these meetings. Due to our growing attendance and lack of space, we added a second worship service in October. We all were amazed at how God was working in us and among us. We ended that year $40,000 over budget, and our regular attendance had grown to ninety. It was obvious to all of us that God truly had called us to this journey of faith, and we were seeing the truth of our obedience.

CHAPTER 18

Growing by Leaps and Bounds

In October 2005, I received a call from Dr. Tim Downs, Conference Minister for the Southeast region of United Church of Christ (UCC) minister (this would be the equivalent of a Bishop in other denominations), asking me to join him and the Reverend Bennie Liggins for coffee. At our meeting, he discussed an interest in beginning conversations with me and our congregation about affiliation. I shared this information with our Vestry and they were very supportive of continuing conversations with Dr. Downs and Reverend Liggins.

In January 2006, I enrolled in the Polity and Theology and History of the UCC class at Vanderbilt. I thoroughly enjoyed the interaction and discussions in the classroom setting. I was amazed at the broad and interesting history of the UCC. What an incredible denomination! The theology, polity, and spiritual struggles of discovering God's truth struck a chord deep within my spirit. I felt a kinship in this history and struggle that is difficult to describe. Somehow these people of faith were honest and courageous enough to struggle to make Christ's love real among all people, pictures, and places of life. This denomination represented on a much larger scale my own experience of reconciling faith. Certainly, there was a broad theological spectrum represented. And, there were parts of the spectrum to which I did not resonate. At the far left end were individuals who could be Unitarian Universalists. At the other end were individuals who would have fit well into the church in which I grew up. The large mass in the middle of the spectrum are who resonated with me most. I found a safeness and warmth that gave me renewed hope for denominational affiliation.

As God continued to work among us at Holy Trinity, we grew in faith and numbers. Our journey of faith continued as we aimed at meeting the new budget and the growing spiritual needs of our family of faith. Our attendance average for 2005 was 120. In December, we saw significant jumps in attendance. Three Sundays we had 140 in attendance. It was obvious we desperately needed more space. We ended the year meeting budget and with renewed excitement; we prayed that God would open doors for us to have our own building.

We had been leasing space from Brookmeade Congregational Church since July 1999. This congregation was a UCC church with a rich history in social justice ministries. They were kind and loving hosts to us. They supported and cheered us on as we began to grow. Holy Trinity Community Church would not be where she is today if it had not been for the grace and kindness of this wonderful congregation. While we may land in different places on the theological spectrum (Brookmeade would fall on the far left of the theological spectrum), we come together at the table as brothers and sisters in Christ. I am very thankful for Rev. Dr. Dan Rosemergy, pastor of the church, who extended an invitation to us in 1999 when we desperately needed a place to meet. He also opened doors and introduced me to his colleagues and the other ministers along the West End corridor. Our little church, which would otherwise have been ostracized from the greater community of faith, had a place because Dan was willing to live out the love of Christ to us and those around him. We participated in the community Thanksgiving service and Good Friday service. Fellowshipping and worshipping with these mainline churches did wonders for our sense of identity. No longer did we see ourselves as a "gay church." We saw ourselves as a vibrant community of faith whose arms were open to anyone who walked in the door.

In early November of 2005, one of the Realtors at Holy Trinity, a dear friend of mine named Steve Deasy, became aware of a church property that was about to go on the market. Located just two miles from Brookmeade Congregational Church, it seemed perfect for our needs at the time. Steve maintained communication with the local Baptist college, who held the deed to the property.

The beginning of December we found out that with assistance from the UCC, we could move forward with purchasing. The week after Christmas there were more than forty individuals who gave more than 800 hours to deep clean the former Horton Heights Free Will Baptist Church which had been empty for nearly a year. To say the least, it was in bad need of cleaning. Our crew came out in force with brooms, mops, Windex, Murphy's Oil soap, vacuum cleaners, carpet and upholstery cleaners, floor cleaners, and buffers. At the end of the week, that building smelled clean and looked pristine.

On January 1, 2006, we had our first worship service at 6727 Charlotte Pike. Initially, we leased the building and property from the Free Will Baptist Foundation in Nashville for $1,000 per month. This was the same rent we had been paying Brookmeade Congregational Church. The plan was to get a loan, which would require a monthly mortgage of $3600. This was an exciting time. However, we all were aware that this was also a step of faith. We trusted that God would grow the church and offerings enough to cover the $3600 monthly mortgage that was coming in July.

This new building brought renewed excitement and growth to the church. Two of the three Sundays in January, we had 140 in attendance and one Sunday we had 160—our highest attendance for a regular service to date. It felt awesome to have our own church building. The pride and ownership I saw among the congregation was incredible. Clearly, we had begun a new chapter in the life of our church.

Our conversations with the UCC continued, and we voted to join this open and affirming denomination. It felt great to have a denominational home with which to affiliate. We were accepted into the Alabama/Tennessee Association of the Southeast Conference of the United Church of Christ in June 2006.

Dr. Downs stepped out in faith with us when he convinced the Southeast Conference Board to hold the mortgage for the building we were buying until we had been in the denomination long enough to hold it ourselves. His willingness to take a chance on me and on us forged a special bond between us that lasts to this day. I'm happy to say that the church experienced significant growth from January 1 to July 1, 2006. When it was time to pay the first month's mortgage, we not only paid it, we were able to start out paying $4600 a month! Seeing God work in and among us in that six-month period did wonders for our spiritual maturity. We were becoming a united body in Christ with a shared vision. And God blessed us as we walked obediently before Him.

The journey from January 2005 to January 2007 prepared us for the bigger steps God would call on us to take. Our unity and focus provided the momentum to continue growing and adding to the church staff. By mid–2007 we had to offer two worship services to accommodate our growth. In the summer of 2008 we added a third service. We had three fifty-five minute services back to back. It was a challenge for me to stay within the allotted time for each service. Somehow, we all worked together to make it happen.

At that time, the Vestry decided we needed to start looking for other property that would allow us to expand. So when any church property or property that could be converted to a church came on the market, our Realtor would let us know. We looked at property within a fifty-to-sixty mile radius of the church. Some of the properties were nice with large sanctuaries. However, they had been built back in the day when most people walked to church. The parking lots for these 500-to-600 seat sanctuaries included 100-120 parking spaces—with no room for expansion. Or, there would be plenty of room to expand, but with Tennessee being full of limestone the blasting required to create more parking would be cost prohibitive. For almost two years, we looked for property and maintained three worship services. Our volunteer real estate scouts were growing weary. And the congregation felt disjointed with three worship services. We wanted to worship as one body of believers.

At the beginning of 2010, I had a conversation with one of the staff members. "What could we build on our current site?" we wondered. The church leadership and I had assumed that expansion would be out of the question with barely three acres. In the next Vestry meeting, we talked about it and decided to order a feasibility study, which would tell us if expansion on our current site was a possibility.

Within three months we had the results of the feasibility study. It indicated that we could build a 500-seat sanctuary, as well as expand the parking area. However, there were additional tests that would be needed to get a more accurate cost: soil boring to check if blasting would be necessary and a topographical survey to indicate the lay of the land and what kind of storm drainage would be required. To everyone's surprise—even the architect's—both tests came back favorable.

Once we began focusing on building on our current site, the consistent signs God gave us were apparent. Everything seemed to point toward staying at our current site and building a new sanctuary. God seemed to be preparing us for very large steps of faith. I think it gave all of us pause. We began lifting our need to God and asking Him to guide us forward. It was an incredibly exciting time, but also a spiritually sobering time when we realized that a building campaign would likely lie ahead. As senior pastor, this was, honestly, the last thing I wanted. I had heard horror stories of building campaigns splitting churches in two. But I also had to recognize and accept that God was clearly pointing us in a particular direction. Before I could lead this congregation forward, I had to have peace with the fact that this was the path God had for me and for all of us. The peace came and we moved forward.

CHAPTER 19

Pain Beyond Words

In the summer of 2005, I received a tearful call from a gay couple in our church. I had known them for several years and considered them dear friends. Dan and Jim were not your stereotypical gay men. Dan had been a fireman, though he now had an office job in accounting. Jim hunted and knew how to "field skin" the game he killed. They both were handsome and quite butch! Dan reminded me of a modern-day Jesus. If I think about Jesus coming to Earth in our time frame, Dan looks and acts like I think Jesus would look and act.

Jim was on the phone asking me if I could meet them at a local park that afternoon. It seemed like an odd request, but I said sure. Jim had been raised conservative Baptist. When he realized he was gay, he did everything he could to fight it, including joining an ex-gay ministry and helping to lead several groups for a while. But there came a time when he realized his sexual orientation was not something he could change. He began doing further study of the Bible and the verses that are so often used to condemn LGBTQ individuals. Through prayer and study, God brought clarity to his spirit. He recognized that the Bible was certainly condemning something in these verses, but it had nothing to do with what we know today as two people of the same sex being in a loving, committed relationship. Once he reconciled his faith and orientation, he began dating Dan. They had been together more than seven years when this nightmare began to unfold.

When I arrived at the park, I spotted them sitting under a tree in the cool summer grass. Jim had his legs crossed, and Dan was leaning over on one hand. They both smiled and thanked me for coming. I told them I was glad to see them. Jim began by saying, "I went home for Father's Day in June to see my parents. My sister, her husband, and their son also came over for lunch. After lunch, I took my nephew, Timmy, down to the creek where I used to play as a child. We caught salamanders. Then we came back to the house and he wanted to throw the football. So I went outside and threw the football with him. I had taken several extra days off to stay with Mom and Dad. On Monday afternoon, my brother-in-law, Darren, pulls into the driveway as I am washing my car and says, 'I know what you did, Jim!' I said, 'What? What on earth are you talking about?' He said, 'I know what you did to my son when you took him to the creek.'"

Jim continued, "I told him…'Yeah, we took our socks and shoes off and walked into the creek. I showed him some crawdads. I caught a salamander for him that he wanted to show his mom. I held the salamander while he played in the water a bit. Then we went to the bank…he put his socks and shoes on. I handed him the salamander, and I put my socks and shoes on and we walked back to the house.'"

By this time, Jim was bawling his eyes out. I told him it was ok and to take his time. He said, "Cindy, my brother-in-law is accusing me of molesting my nephew while we were at the creek. As God as my witness, I am not that kind of man. I would never do anything like that to my nephew."

I said, "How old is your nephew and what is he saying?"

Jim said, "He is five-and-a-half, and I have no idea what he is saying. All I got was the visit from my brother-in-law, who is extremely homophobic."

I said, "So what is your sister saying?"

"She's so submissive to her husband—anything he says she just agrees with."

I asked if he had been able to talk to his sister. He said yes, but just briefly. I asked again what she said. Jim said, "She said that her husband had taken their son into his room when they got home and talked to him. He came out of Timmy's room livid, saying that Jim had touched Timmy in a bad way." I asked if his sister had been able to talk with her son. Jim had asked her that and her response was, "Jim, I can't ask him those kind of perverted questions. This is already going to hurt him and may make him gay, like you." Jim was dumbfounded by his sister's ignorance. She was a school teacher. Her husband was an attorney. They were well-educated people. But both were very homophobic.

Jim said, "I told my brother-in-law that as God was my witness, I did not touch Timmy at all except when I handed him the salamander to hold while I put my shoes and socks on."

The brother-in-law got back in his car and said before pulling out of the driveway, "Jim, this is not over! You will be hearing more from me." Jim went inside his parents' house and tried his best to share what had just happened. His mother immediately began to cry and called Jim's sister. Beth told her mother the same thing she told Jim, "Timmy's daddy had taken Timmy into his room when they got home and then came out livid, saying Jim had touched Timmy." When her mother asked if she had talked to Timmy, she got the same response, "I can't ask him those perverted questions. I'm just worried he's going to end up gay now, like Jim."

Jim's mother hung up the phone, dazed. Jim's father began questioning him in detail about the time that he and Timmy spent at the creek. They were gone about forty-five minutes. His dad asked over and over again, "Jim, you are sure that you did not touch Timmy in an inappropriate way while you were at the creek? Even, just some kind of horseplay?" Jim told his dad exactly what they did and that he had only touched Timmy when he handed him the salamander to hold while he put his shoes and socks on.

Jim's dad called his son-in-law. He asked him specifically what his grandson had said about being touched. The son-in-law said, "Your faggot son touched my son and he's going to pay!" Again, Jim's dad asked exactly what his grandson had said about being touched. The son-in-law never answered the question, but kept repeating that Jim had molested his son and he was going to pay. Jim's dad hung up the phone and asked Jim to again recount the story of taking his nephew to the creek. Jim told the story yet again. His dad shook his head and began to cry. "Dear Lord, what is going on here?" he said. "I wish I could talk to Timmy. Darren wouldn't say what Timmy said. I'd like to hear Timmy's version of this story."

His mother piped up and said, "Yes, Beth hasn't talked to Timmy either." At this point, Jim's dad drove over to his daughter's home. He knocked on the door and was met by Darren, who refused to let him in the house. He explained that he just wanted to know that Timmy was ok. That he would like to talk to him." Darren once again told his father-in-law that his son was a faggot who molested his five-year-old son. When Jim Sr. asked again specifically what Timmy said, Darren said, "This conversation is over. Your son is going to pay for this. He will be hearing more from me. I am filing charges against him." Darren then slammed the door in Jim Sr.'s face. Jim Sr. tried to call his daughter on her cell phone, but she did not answer. He left a message pleading with her to talk to Timmy alone, without Darren present. She never returned the call.

Jim drove back to Nashville in emotional knots. He had gone home to be with his father and family for Father's Day. He had known that his brother-in-law was homophobic. But, he had never imagined Darren was capable of something like this. Jim contacted an attorney as soon as he got home. His mother called him and told him that she had gone over to Beth and Darren's but that Darren would not let her come inside. "Jim," she said, "you better get a lawyer. I'm afraid of what Darren is trying to do to you." Jim assured his mother that he had already spoken with an attorney. Jim had tried to go to work on the morning he called me. He went into his office but could not concentrate. He called Dan and said he was calling me.

As I listened to Jim's story I felt a sickness in the pit of my stomach. I knew Jim and I knew he was not the kind of man to touch or harm a child. I looked him straight in the eyes and said, "Jim, I believe you. I know you, and I know you are not that kind of man." I went over and hugged him, and he wept like a baby in my arms.

I asked him what the attorney had said and he replied, "She said if he filed charges, the arraignment would be sent to the police office in my county. They would pick me up and transport me to the county jail in Georgia." I asked if there was anything he could do in the meantime. The attorney had told him that his brother-in-law may well have just been making empty threats. Jim said he doubted it. I held Dan and Jim's hands and prayed for the Spirit of God to intervene. I asked God to manifest the truth in this situation and to strengthen and uphold Jim during this time. I asked God to be present and give Jim peace and to allow him to lean into God's grace and promises. I read several passages of Scripture to Dan and Jim and reminded them that we serve a God who is faithful.

One month passed, then two, and Jim started to think that, perhaps, his brother-in-law had been making empty threats. Jim's parents told him that Darren no longer allowed them to come to their home. He also did not allow his wife or their son to visit Jim's parents. They were devastated beyond words at not being able to see their grandson. They had no idea what Darren had told the child, but he was obviously controlling all the strings.

It was at the end of the third month when the county police knocked on Jim's door with an arrest warrant.

Darren had filed formal charges stating that Jim had molested five-year-old Timmy on Father's Day. Jim went into an emotional tailspin. Dan was not home from work yet, and the officers would not allow him to make a call. He jotted a quick note saying he was being taken to the county jail. That evening when Dan got home and Jim's car was in the driveway but Jim was nowhere to be found, he came across the note in Jim's handwriting saying, "Darren has filed charges. I have been arrested. I am in the county jail. They will be taking me to the county jail in Georgia on Monday." As soon as Dan read the note, he called me. My blood boiled. How could someone do something like this? Jim loved God and was an amazing example of what a Christian should be.

I went to their home, and Dan and I drove to the county jail. They would not let Dan see Jim because they were not married. But I, as his minister, had visitation rights. Dan wanted to make sure I gave Jim his Bible. They walked me through a few gates and motioned toward a chair that faced a glass pane. I took a seat; there was phone receiver at my side. I saw Jim being escorted to this area. I saw them remove his hand cuffs. He walked over and sat down. He had no words. He was in shock, as anyone would be. He just looked into my eyes and tears streamed down his face. I picked up the receiver, and he picked up his receiver. I said, "Jim, you are not alone. God is right here with you. He is as close as your next breath. I am going to walk with you and do whatever I can to help you. They wouldn't let Dan come back, but he wants you to know that he loves you. He wants you to know that he is going to be in touch with your parents and with the police departments. He's going to see if he can drive you to Georgia and let you turn yourself in there. He is on the phone with your attorney right now. We are going to do everything we can. But, please remember, you are not alone. God's holy angels are surrounding you in these moments."

I asked the guard to please give Jim his Bible and he did. I told him that his Bible was worn from where he had studied and used it over the years. I said, "Jim, find those promises and hold fast to them. God is here. And you are going to get through this. Jim, I love you. You are not alone." And with that, the guard said my time was up. I watched as they handcuffed Jim and escorted him away. He looked back at me, holding his Bible under his arm.

The county police held him until Monday. They would not release him. They made it clear that they would be escorting him to Georgia. It was obvious by the way they were responding that they saw Jim as a pedophile who molested his nephew. They saw and treated him as guilty because he was a gay man. I don't understand these injustices in any way. I know the LGBTQ community is certainly not the first or only minority who has faced injustice. But seeing it up close and personal made me so incredibly angry—a righteous anger that makes you cry out to God to make things right.

Jim was transported to Georgia on Monday, but he could not be released until he had a bond hearing in which the judge set bail. It didn't matter that Jim's father went down to the jail and said, "Name the price...I want my son out of there." They simply told him his son could not be released until the bond hearing, which would be on Thursday. Jim Sr. was so angry. He wanted to drive straight to his daughter's house and confront his son-in-law. But he did not want to make things worse for Jim, so he cried and prayed all the way home.

Dan had called to let me know when the hearing would be and where it would be held. He said, "Cindy, I hate to ask you this, but I know it would mean the world to Jim if you were there when he gets out." I told Dan there was no other place I would rather be than there to give Jim a big hug.

I woke bright and early on Thursday morning and made the five-hour drive to rural Georgia. When I arrived, Jim's parents hugged me and were so appreciative that I had made the trip down. I told them I was thrilled to be able to do this for Jim. I knew he was innocent, and I wanted to do whatever I could to support him. We weren't able to be in the court room, so we watched on a monitor as Jim stood before the judge and declared his innocence. The judge set the bail, and about an hour later, Jim walked through the double doors with the work clothes he had worn the Friday before. He was so glad to be free. He gave us all a big smile before breaking down and crying in his dad's arms. We all surrounded them and held on to them.

Finally, Jim said, "I'm starving! The food wasn't very good, and I haven't really had much of an appetite." His mother told him that she had cooked his favorite meal. We went to their home and enjoyed the warm hospitality. Before I left, we got in a circle and I prayed for Jim, for Dan, for Jim Sr., and Jim's Mom. I prayed for Jim's sister and brother-in-law, asking God to move in ways that only He can do. I asked God to protect Jim as he moved forward in this unfolding and unpredictable situation.

At church on Sunday, I was so glad to see Jim and Dan in their usual seats. They both, as usual, had their worn Bibles in hand. These men truly loved God and walked with Him. Why God, I thought, do You allow these kinds of things to happen? I knew God did not cause this situation. I just didn't understand—and still don't understand—why He sometimes allows us to walk through the fire. What I do know, beyond a shadow of a doubt, is that God is good and He can bring about good out of the darkest circumstances if we invite Him into them. And I know He gives us the grace and strength to face these kind of nightmares that sometimes come into our lives. I knew Jim and Dan were walking forward by the grace of God. I knew that God was present. I could feel His mighty Presence in and around Jim and Dan.

As Jim moved forward, he and his attorney could get little information about a trial date. Jim stayed in touch with his parents. He realized just how hate-filled his brother-in-law was when his Dad told him about trying to reach out one more time to his son-in-law and sister. What followed was a message from his son-in-law saying that Timmy had also mentioned that his grandfather had also touched him inappropriately. He told Jim Sr. and his wife to stay out of their lives if he didn't want to face what Jim was facing.

The New Year came, but there was little celebrating for Jim and Dan. Both knew that Jim could face a trial in the coming months, and depending on the jury could be found guilty and sentenced to jail. The thought of that weighed heavily on both of them.

In March of 2007, I received a call from Dan telling me that Jim had been having some health issues. He had gone to the doctor and the doctor had ordered some tests. The preliminary results were that Jim had cancer—liver cancer. It was clear to me that the intense stress this man had been under had compromised his health. Two weeks later, an oncologist confirmed that Jim did, indeed, have liver cancer, and it was an aggressive form. There were some treatment options available; however, given the type of cancer. the odds of the treatments making a big difference were slim. With that news, Jim decided to forgo treatments. He went to his work and immediately filled out the paperwork for short-term disability. He wanted to enjoy the time he had left with Dan.

When I got the news that Jim had terminal cancer [at the age of 40] and had just a few months to live, I was devastated. I loved this man and his partner. I knew God's grace had been sustaining them in this nightmare they had been facing for nearly a year. As I tried to comprehend this information, God reminded me that He is good and gracious. In my visits with Jim and Dan, their faith never wavered. One night Dan pulled me aside and said, "Cindy, I believe God is being merciful to Jim and taking him on home to heaven. He has been through so much. It's like God is saying, 'Enough!' and freeing Jim from this nightmare." I told Dan there was something really comforting about his words. There I was, the minister, being ministered to by a parishioner.

The beginning of May, Jim had to go into the hospital. He was getting much weaker and sicker. He was having a more difficult time keeping food down. I went by to visit him. I walked in the room and I said, "Jim, how are you doing?"

He said without batting an eye, "I know Jesus Christ as my personal Savior, and I am ready to meet Him!"

I said, "Jim, that is going to be an amazing experience! To actually meet Jesus face to face." A nurse came in and interrupted our conversation. While she was taking some blood, Jim's parents walked in the room. What a wonderful surprise!

Dan had called them and let them know that Jim was in the hospital and getting weaker. He wanted to have a conversation with Jim about being transferred to hospice. He thought it would go better if Jim's parents were present. Dan leaned over and asked me to stay with them. Jim's parents told him about the trip up to Nashville. It was quite a long ride for them. Then the conversation turned to Jim's health. His mother said, "Dan told me you were getting weaker and having a hard time keeping food down."

"Yes," Jim said, "I'm definitely getting weaker."

His dad chimed in, "Son, have you thought about going into hospice?"

Oh, dear Lord! I thought Jim was going to come out of the bed and hurt someone. "I will just tell all of you, I am not going into hospice!" he said. "The money in my savings account is not going to be used for that!"

His mother calmed him down and said, "Jim, we love you and just want to help."

Little did we know that this would be the last conversation we would have with Jim. Jim's parents and I hugged him and said goodbye. Dan was staying overnight with him. We hugged Dan and told both of them we would see them tomorrow.

Dan called me before 6 the next morning to say that Jim had passed. He told me that the nurse had awakened them both when she came in around 3:30 to check Jim's blood pressure, but they both had fallen back to asleep quickly. Dan woke around 5:30 and looked over at Jim. He was slumped over in the bed. He jumped up and felt him. He was cold.

Dan was obviously shaken to his core. He had called Jim's parents before calling me. They really hadn't talked to Jim much about a funeral or where he would like to be buried. I could tell as I asked Dan questions that it was all too overwhelming for him.

"Dan," I said, "what if I meet you and Jim's parents for breakfast and we make a plan for the day? I know many of the mortuaries in Nashville. If I can talk to you all, we can figure out what would be best for you and Jim's parents." He sounded so relieved when I offered this.

"Thanks you so much, Cindy! I have never done anything like this and it all just seems so overwhelming right now."

At breakfast Dan said, "You know, I think Jim just decided he was going to go on now, rather than later. He was adamant that he wanted his savings and retirement to be split between me and you all. You know how he is. I think he just told God, 'Please, just come on and take me.' And God did." They all laughed while I smiled. It seems one of the things I didn't really know about Jim was that he was a penny pincher. And he was not about to let his savings be squandered on staying in a residential hospice facility. He obviously had a talk with God and told God he was ready to meet Jesus. And God granted his wish.

Once all the plans for picking up Jim's body and arranging for the time frames of visitation and the funeral were in place, we went to lunch. Dan and Jim's parents seemed so relieved to have made some decisions. I began to talk to them about the actual service. They all agreed that Jim loved some of the older hymns. We chose several of them. Then Dan asked if I thought there was any possibility of the church choir singing at the service. I told him I wasn't sure, but that I would make some calls. Jim and Dan were a well-loved couple in our church. I knew if there was any way their schedules would allow, the choir members would love to be a part of remembering Jim. And, sure enough, every single one made arrangements to be present and sing at Jim's funeral.

Jim's mom wondered out loud to her husband, "Do you think we need to call Beth?" Jim Sr. told her he felt it would best not to make a call to Jim's sister. He said, "She can read the obituary in the paper." I could tell this whole situation was so painful for these dear parents. Here they were planning their son's funeral all the while knowing they couldn't call his sister and share the news with her. In the last year, they had lost their daughter and grandson and seen their son be wrongly accused of sexually molesting his nephew. The lies, hate, and deceit from their son-in-law had torn the very fabric of their hearts and family. And there was little they could do because the family was prominent in their small town. (Darren owned a large law firm.) Everything that was dear to them had been ripped from their lives. But in the midst of these huge losses and pain, they still trusted God and found their strength in Him.

Jim's mother told a story of her son getting off the bus from school in the pouring rain. "He didn't have his coat on, but had it under his arm," she said. "I said, 'Jim, what on earth are you doing? It is pouring rain outside. I bought you that coat to use!' He walked into the kitchen and opened the coat up to show me something he had made for me in his pottery class! I felt like the worst mother ever!"

Then Jim's dad told us the story of when Jim was a teenager and he caught him smoking. He said, "I went to the store and bought two packs of cigarettes and two packs of Skoal. I was going to teach that boy a lesson! I got him in the truck and drove us down by the creek. I lit a cigarette and made Jim smoke it! I made him put the Skoal in his mouth and smoke one cig after another. He opened the truck door and started throwing up. As soon as he was finished, I just handed him another cigarette. I'll have to say, there was never a problem with any tobacco products after that." We all laughed at the thought of Jim smoking two packs of cigarettes and chewing snuff.

Jim's mother all of a sudden had a worried look on her face. "Jim," she said, "what if people from our church come to the funeral?" She looked at me and said, "No one in our church knew about Jim and Dan. We loved Jim because he was our son. But, some of these folks don't know about this and they may have an issue with it."

He said, "Honey, if they can't love us like we loved our son and support us in our time of grief, that's just too bad. We have been through way too much to worry about what they may think or say. God has brought us this far and He sure isn't going to abandon us now. God will take care of those people."

And, sure enough, God did. The chapel was packed. About half those in attendance were from Jim's parents' church. And I'm guessing they were getting the show of their life! Here's a woman preaching the sermon! God forbid. And some of these men are a bit effeminate. And some of these women look like Larry the Cable Guy. Yep, there were some looks throughout the visitation and service. The entire service focused on Jesus Christ and the faith Jim had in Him. The choir sang with such energy and passion I wanted to jump up and shout. And I did my best to remember Jim as the wonderfully loving, funny and faith-filled man that he was. Interestingly, a number of couples from Jim's parents' church came forward and told me how much they appreciated the message and the beautiful music. Somehow, God had once again inhabited our worship and lifted all of us above this difficult circumstance. We had seen Jesus Christ lifted high, and God had touched hearts in ways that He can only do.

I'm sad to say that Jim's parents still do not have a relationship with their daughter, Beth. Since Jim's death in June 2006, she has given birth to a daughter. Jim's mom saw Beth walking into the grocery store with the beautiful granddaughter she has never met. Her heart bleeds over this loss. She and Jim Sr. continue to pray that God will bring restoration to their family and that Jim's name will be vindicated in time.

Rev. Cyd Andrews-Looper

CHAPTER 20

The Man I Called Daddy

In May of 2009, I received a call from my mother saying my daddy had pulled a knife on her. It was clear something serious was going on. That event led me to move my dad to Nashville. My mom was afraid to live with him alone. After a series of neurological tests and psychological evaluations, he was diagnosed with negative pressure hydrocephalus, dementia, and severe depression. The father that I had grown up with—the father I knew and loved—was no longer there. This man had angry outbursts, fell regularly, cried often, and suffered from paranoia.

I kept Daddy in my home for almost two months. I quickly realized his condition was more than I could care for—even with home health. I made the very difficult decision, with the input of my mother, sister, and brother, to place Daddy in a nursing home. It was one of the most difficult, if not the most difficult, decisions I have ever faced.

I sat down with Daddy and tried to explain the situation. He was lucid enough to argue with me. And then he began to cry. Nothing has been more heart-wrenching in my life than sitting before my daddy, watching him weep like a baby, and listening to him beg to simply go home to South Carolina. Driving him to the nursing home and leaving him there that afternoon truly broke something inside me.

I had only heard about individuals having to make these difficult decisions for aging parents. Never had I dreamed that I would be faced with this excruciatingly painful scenario. Certainly, I had talked with parishioners who were facing the issues related to aging parents. For whatever reason, I think I assumed my parents would simply drop dead of heart attacks…since heart disease is so prevalent in my family. There were no easy answers. My mother was genuinely afraid of him. He had mistreated home health workers and asked them to leave. The atmosphere he created was hostile at best and unstable and unsafe at worst. I simply could not let him go back to South Carolina. And I could not care for him in my home. The only safe option for him and his family was a nursing home setting.

I talked with the social worker at the nursing home at length. She was so kind, loving, and helpful. She knew well the difficulty family members had in making the decision that I had to make. She assured me they would take excellent care of Daddy.

I committed to visiting Daddy as often as I possibly could. The nursing home was forty-five minutes from my home and thirty-five minutes from the church. I tried to visit as least every other day. And whatever Daddy asked for, I did my best to get. He wanted a glass of wine every night before he went to bed. I spoke with the social worker and doctors and they agreed it would not harm him. I would just have to purchase the wine and they would give it to him nightly. So I did that. He wanted a television and radio. I purchased both and had cable set up in his room. He wanted a small refrigerator in which to keep fruit. I got that and kept it stocked with his favorites: grapes, nectarines, and cherries.

I tried at least once a week to take Daddy out to a local restaurant. Because he could not walk long distances, I borrowed a wheel chair. I took him to the park and to the mall as well as to other places I knew he would enjoy. He was always happy and smiling when I arrived. But when it was time for me to leave, he would begin crying.

Within a month, he began acting out violently and exhibiting signs of deep depression. The social worker called one morning to let me know they were referring him to the local psych hospital. I met him there and had him admitted. The physicians at the nursing home had tried to adjust his psych and depression meds, but couldn't find a combination that worked. Daddy was in the psych hospital for six weeks before he returned to the nursing home. During that time, Mom was paying for his room so he could return to this facility. This was one of the better nursing homes in Nashville. She had long-term care insurance, but it did not pay for the first six weeks of stay. Mom had to pay for that out of pocket. Unfortunately, Mom and Daddy had not prepared to cover this cost when they took out the policies. It became a financial strain for Mom until the policy went into effect. And, on top of that, the policy would not cover the nursing home cost while Daddy was in the psych hospital. Mom ended up having to pay thousands of dollars. It pretty much depleted their small amount of savings.

Daddy stayed in the nursing home for another three months before being referred once again to the psych hospital. This time, Mom said she could not pay to keep his room. We would just have to find another facility when he got out.

He ended up being in the psych hospital another six weeks. From the time I first placed Daddy in the nursing home, Mom made the seven-hour drive monthly to visit him. But every time he saw her, he became very angry. He told her he wanted a divorce and that she would get nothing. This was incredibly difficult for her and for him. So we decided that for a while it would be best if she didn't visit. My brother, who also lived in South Carolina, did bring his family up to visit with Daddy. One of Daddy's joys was seeing his grandchildren. So that visit certainly brightened his outlook.

Over and over again, he would tell us he simply wanted to go home. And when we would try to think of possible ways to make that happen, my mother would become very fearful. She simply was not in a place emotionally to deal with his abusive behavior and words. So my brother and I finally had to tell Daddy that going home to South Carolina was not an option. At first he was weepy and despondent. Then he became angry and decided he was going to fight this decision. Daddy would have moments of lucidity that would make me question my decisions. But when I observed him over a week or more, I knew there were serious things going on.

In one of his lucid moments, he contacted a lawyer and told him he wanted to get out of the nursing home. He happened to be in the psych hospital when the lawyer first visited him. I asked that the facility do a competency exam on Daddy. If he was indeed competent to make his own decision, I would certainly allow him to do so. My brother and I met with the psychiatrist and he explained that the executive functioning of Daddy's brain was not working, and neither was the part that allowed him to rationalize. So he literally could not comprehend why his family would be keeping him in a nursing home. In his mind, there was nothing wrong with him, other than the physical changes that had occurred from aging. Daddy was, indeed, not competent. The doctor tried to explain this to Daddy, who was convinced that my brother and I had met with and brainwashed the doctor. Daddy insisted on pursuing a legal route to get out of the nursing home.

I called my attorney and got an emergency petition of the court to have Daddy declared temporarily incompetent. Once he was well enough, he would go to a nursing home. But the family was going to have to go to court and have him legally declared incompetent. The thought of what this process was going to do to Daddy, to Mom, to me, and to my brother and sister made me very depressed and discouraged. Fortunately, I was blessed with a supportive partner who got me through some dark nights of the soul. And, thankfully, I have a strong faith and reliance upon God. This situation pushed me to emotional and spiritual limits that I had never faced. And, in all honesty, I hope I never have to again.

When January came, Daddy was placed in the only nursing home that was available at the time. It was an hour and a half away. I went to the facility with Daddy's things and met with the staff. I tried to communicate what my daddy meant to me and how hard it was to see him in this condition. They were very loving and assured me they would take good care of him. I was anxious because I knew I would not be able to visit him as often because of the distance—and because I was having major surgery in two weeks with a recovery time of six weeks.

In addition to the heart-wrenching challenges surrounding my dad, my partner's father had cancer. He had been fighting the disease for nearly three years. At the beginning of January, he was officially diagnosed with leukemia. The doctors had told him that once that diagnoses came, the treatment options would be limited, mainly because of his age.

So 2010 began with my partner and I watching our fathers become men we no longer recognized. It was a painful time for everyone. I visited with my Daddy on Friday, February 12. Little did I know that, as I hugged Daddy goodbye that day, it would be the last time I would see him alive. The weight of this entire situation was much bigger than me. I had no choice but to give it to God.

CHAPTER 21

What a Way to Start a New Year!

In 2009, I had made the decision to have gastric bypass surgery the following year. I realized that my extra weight was causing many health problems—high blood pressure, diabetes, sleep apnea, etc.

I saw myself just where my father was when he was my age. I knew if I didn't get control of my weight, my health would decline just as his had. It took me two years to make the decision. But I finally had the surgery scheduled for the February 15, 2010. My recovery time would be six weeks. When I saw my Dad on February 12, I knew that it would be at least a month before I could visit again. I was excited about the surgery and ready to be in a healthier place physically. But, I was also worried about him being alone in this nursing home. I asked God to be with him and comfort him.

I had to be at the hospital early on Monday morning. My son was out of school for an in-service day, so he and my partner sat in the waiting room during my surgery. After surgery, I was disoriented and in a lot of pain. The surgery had been performed by laparoscopy, so they only had to make six small incisions across my abdomen. One on the left side especially painful.

My son and Leigh were in the room when I arrived. It was so good to see them. Leigh's mom came later in the afternoon to get my son, and my partner spent the night with me. It was a difficult night for her and me. I was in pain and could not rest. She was trying to be present and get me anything I needed.

The next morning they took blood and discovered that my potassium had dropped significantly. Right away they had me drinking liquid potassium, which has got to be some of the most horrid tasting stuff I've ever had! The next day, my potassium was still low, and I could not be released until it was in a normal range. I ended up spending three nights and four days in the hospital. To say the least, when I got home to my own bed, I was thrilled.

Leigh had prepared our entire second floor to accommodate my needs. There was a small refrigerator and microwave in our rec room, along with my protein drinks and powders. I had to be on a liquid protein diet for two weeks. And I had to drink sixty-four ounces of water in addition to drinking fifty to sixty grams of protein. My stomach had gone from the size of a football to the size of a half dollar. Small sips were difficult for my small pouch to receive. I would have moments of nausea. And was getting so tired of drinking every meal. It was a challenge to do everything the doctor wanted, but I did my best.

I went for my one-week checkup and all reports were good. I was taking my supplements, drinking my protein and liquids, walking up and down the hall. I had lost twenty pounds since the surgery. This rapid weight loss is not unusual. The surgery and the regimen that follows is designed to get the weight off and keep it off. Wow, the weight was really coming off!

The next week was a bit better. I was less sore and could drink small sips without pain or nausea. I still just wanted to bite into a big juicy hamburger. Not to gorge myself—I just really wanted to chew food and swallow it. But I knew it was important to allow my pouch to heal. Otherwise, I could have serious problems later.

By the beginning of the third week, I felt more hopeful. I was now allowed very soft foods like Greek yogurt and cottage cheese. Still, I had to get fifty to sixty grams of protein, at least, each day. It was a welcome sensation to have something other than liquid stimulating my taste buds. I spoke with Daddy by phone on Tuesday. It was good to hear his voice. He was relieved that I was on my way to recovery. He asked when I was coming to visit him. I told him I hoped to feel strong enough by the following Saturday to make the trip out.

He also told me, as I was already aware, that the court date for the competency hearing was Monday, March 15. We both cried as we talked about this difficult situation. We ended by telling each other how much we loved each other and acknowledging that God was holding our family close. That would be the last conversation I would have with Daddy.

On Friday, March 5 at 7:36 a.m., I received a phone call from the nursing home. The nurse simply said, "We think your dad has had a massive stroke. He has no heartbeat and is not breathing." I could not ask her to confirm what I knew to be true. My father was dead. Leigh loaded me in the car and we made the long hour-and-a-half trip to Erin, Tennessee. The nurse had told me they were taking Daddy to the local emergency room. I walked into the small rural hospital and gave them my name and my dad's name.

They told me to have a seat and they would be right with me. About 20 minutes had passed when a nurse and doctor came into the waiting room. The doctor spoke slowly and explained that Daddy had simply fallen back and collapsed. He took several shallow breaths and stopped breathing. He had passed very peacefully. I told the doctor I wanted to see him.

Upon hearing that my Daddy was dead, I went emotionally numb. My father, the man whom I adored growing up, was gone. I would never be able to hug him or have a conversation with him again on this earth. In that moment, I also knew where his soul was…it was with God. Daddy no longer was in pain. He no longer was confused. He no longer was depressed. Daddy was whole, at peace, and in the presence of the Divine love of the Creator who had made him.

Leigh walked into the small room with me, along with the nurse. Daddy's body was covered with a sheet. The nurse removed it from his face. As a minister, I had seen dozens of dead bodies. But when it is your own flesh and blood that you're looking at, it is much more difficult. I hugged him and sobbed as I had not cried in a very long time. He truly looked peaceful with his eyes closed. I knew his soul was flying free now. I knew he understood all things now.

This man, who had been an amazing father, was gone. And from here, part of my job was to make sure he was remembered well. I called my brother, who wanted to drive to Mom's house to tell her in person. I called my brother-in-law so he could tell my sister. The shock of Daddy's death began to set in, I went into this robotic emotional state. I almost think it is God's way of allowing us to face incredibly painful situations.

Though I felt emotionally numb, I felt God's Presence in such a powerful way. Once Mom was informed, I called her minister to make funeral arrangements. I went to the local funeral home to make arrangements for Daddy's body to be flown to South Carolina. I had to make calls to my son's school, to begin planning the funeral service, and so on. I knew my Daddy better than anyone, and I wanted him to be remembered for all the things I loved about him.

I debated on whether to preach on Sunday. But as I thought about it, I felt one of the best ways to honor my father would be to do what God had called me to do: to lift up the good news of the gospel—to give testimony of God's grace and Presence in the midst of challenging moments. I felt the power and Presence of the Holy Spirit in such an amazing way throughout our three services that Sunday. I literally felt carried by a power and strength beyond my own. I was absolutely empty. But God had filled me with a grace and love that overflowed. It was truly a time when heaven came down to earth. Our entire congregation was blessed and uplifted by the abiding Presence of God.

I left with my son and partner after the third service to drive to South Carolina. We arrived around 8:00 that evening. The funeral was on Monday afternoon. We had decided to schedule the visitation two hours before the funeral. I was amazed at the literally hundreds of people who came through the line. I had not seen some of these individuals for more than twenty years. They were all so loving and kind.

As they closed the casket and we prepared to move to the chapel, I gathered with the other ministers. My parents were members of an Independent Baptist Church that clearly did not believe that God called women to ministry. Two of the ministers on staff would speak and then I would give the final eulogy. How were these ministers going to act? How was this congregation going to respond? Again, I gave all it all to God, trusting that the Spirit would move among us and bring peace.

Thankfully, the congregation received my words warmly, as I remembered the father I had been blessed with as a child. Again, as we were having lunch at Mom's church following the funeral, I stood amazed at what God's grace and Presence can and will do if we will simply relinquish our concerns. My son, partner and I were loved and received in these moments. It was either ignorance or the grace of God! Either way, I thanked God for it.

As I look back at the events of early 2010 I see so clearly the grace and mercy of God in my life and my family's life. God was merciful to take my Daddy before he had to appear before a judge and be declared legally incompetent. God was merciful to spare him the humiliation. God was full of grace and mercy toward my family in giving us the wisdom, strength, and faith to get through these excruciatingly painful moments.

I once again affirm with confidence that God is good and loving. God is my strong tower and deliverer. I can trust God with every aspect of my life and the life of my family.

CHAPTER 22

My Daddy's Gift to Me

About a month following my Daddy's death, I was consumed by guilt. The events of the previous year in which I had to make excruciatingly painful decisions concerning Daddy were killing my heart. I kept envisioning him crying and begging me to let him go home to S.C. I felt like the worst person on the earth. While I knew he was in heaven and no longer in pain, the guilt I felt for putting him in a nursing home and having to begin the process of having him declared legally incompetent was filling my soul with a heaviness and a darkness. The weight of it seemed to grow daily.

My Daddy came to me one night in a dream. There was a giant vertical sphere that was clear and iridescent at the same time and I was inside it. I saw souls rising and some coming down and hovering a bit. I felt myself rising slowly upward. Then a soul was descending just as slowly and it stopped right in front of me. The other souls continued to ascend and descend around us. I looked at this soul that had stopped in front of me and it was my Daddy's face. He looked me in the eyes and said, "Cindy, all is well. You are well. I am well. We are well." He smiled at me and then began ascending with the other souls going up. A peace came over me in that dream for which I have no words.

When I woke the next morning, I remembered the dream vividly. I felt such a conscious peace as I reflected on it. My Daddy visited me in my dream in order to bring me assurance that he understood all the decisions I had to make when he was on earth in his physical body. He visited me to bring me peace and comfort. From that day forward, I never had guilt again. I became aware for the first time in my life (at the age of 48) that our loved one can and will visit us when they have passed. We just have to be open to receiving.

CHAPTER 23

The Losses Continue...

Leigh's dad was diagnosed with pre-leukemia in 2005. He was diagnosed with leukemia in January of 2010. From there he began to experience serious decline. By summer he was in and out of the hospital. By late summer, he had contracted a serious bacterial infection that required hospitalization. He came home for a short time before going back into the hospital with pneumonia. On September 15, 2010, the Rev. Dr. J. L. A. went to be with the Lord. He had preached and ministered in the local church and served as Vice President of the Southern Baptist Convention for more than fifty years. This man of God left an amazing legacy of faith and love. He was not your typical Southern Baptist minister. When Leigh came out to him, he told her, "This is not an issue for me. I love you and will always love you." Dr. A. was one of the kindest and most loving men I've known. He had integrity, character, and wisdom. He wasn't afraid of showing his sensitive side. He loved art, played the piano amazingly well, dressed immaculately, and could preach an amazing sermon. I am thankful that my life was touched by his life and ministry.

As with my family, Leigh was a bit concerned about her family's reaction to me at the funeral. Hayden and I were there by her side as they were for me. My partner's mom asked me to give a prayer at the funeral service. This was one of the greatest honors I have had in my ministry.

Being included in this sacred and holy service, where so many Southern Baptist leaders and friends were present, was such a loving gesture to my partner and me. Somehow, we both felt the incredible love and grace of God overflowing in our lives. For God was doing something only God could do—changing the hearts of individuals and bringing light and understanding. We were among God's people and all seemed well and holy. Thanks be to God!

In the year that followed, my partner and I had to face all the "firsts" without our fathers—the first Thanksgiving, Christmas, birthday, Father's Day. That first year that follows the death of a loved one is the most difficult as we adjust to their absence. I remembered the one-year anniversary of my Daddy's death by going home and participating in the funeral of his brother. Ironically, he was buried on the same day Daddy was a year before. There was something comforting about being with family and being reminded that our loved ones are in heaven and at peace.

One of the things I have learned through all of this is that we only have today. Certainly, we can and should plan for tomorrow. But we need to be present in the moment. As difficult as the moments sometimes can be, if we allow God to be present, we will get through them. My faith has grown deeper because I've experienced God literally carrying me spiritually when I could not carry myself. I've realized that when all I have is God that God is enough. From mid–2007 to the summer of 2011 I felt like I was facing a spiritual and emotional "threshing floor" experience. I hold "things" much more loosely today. I've been reminded that I have a certain amount of time on this earth. And I can spend that time on temporal things—things that will pass—or I can spend that time on things that have eternal value. I hold my family and friends much more closely today.

The Spirit has affirmed the truth to me that the law of God is simple. Love God and love others. That law has eternal value. I will never regret anything done in the name of love for God or for others.

Rev. Cyd Andrews-Looper

CHAPTER 24

Daddy, Is That You?

About a month after Leigh's Dad died, it was a difficult time for both of us. I started walking in the morning because I had almost lost all my weight and the exercise helped that and my stress. One morning, there was a dove next to my Forerunner that followed me out to the sidewalk. The next morning, again, that same dove was beside my SUV…and again, it followed me out to the sidewalk. The third morning, the same thing. By the fourth morning, when the dove was beside my vehicle and following me to the sidewalk, it had my attention. I stopped and looked at it. It then took a few steps toward me and stopped, then just looked at me. In that moment, I remembered how much my Daddy loved doves. I said, "Daddy, is that you?" The dove looked at me and tilted its little head and took another step toward me. I began crying. "Daddy, it is you. You have been trying to get my attention, haven't you?" The dove continued to just look at me. We had about two minutes of just looking into each other's eyes in the stillness of the morning air. Then, the dove flew away. There was something so comforting about that experience.

The next morning I walked out to the driveway and sure enough, there was the dove again. I said, "Hi Daddy! Thank you for being persistent and getting my attention. You brought me such comfort yesterday." The dove then flew away.

I didn't see a dove again until the following spring. I was sitting on my bed on Sunday morning before church drinking my protein shake and reading through my sermon. I looked out the window and on the window sill were two doves!! Not one, but two! Daddy knew that the week prior had been a challenging one for me. Pastoring a church brings unique challenges that only another pastor can understand. But, my Daddy knew and he visited me with two doves that Sunday morning to let me know that he was present to love and support me in my physical journey on this earth.

It was the visits from my Daddy in dreams and through doves that put me in touch with the unseen spiritual realm that is the only true reality. From these experiences, I began to study and become more aware of the role of angels and loved ones who have passed. I have found great comfort in the visits of my Daddy and brought great comfort to others whom I encouraged to look for messages from their loved ones who have passed. Our loved ones will communicate with us if we are open to receiving them.

CHAPTER 25

Have You Ever Met Crazy?

The following story is true. I could not have made it up if I tried. I wanted to include it in memory of my friend and former parishioner, Billy Ray Baker!

A man that had been part of the congregation since the very first month became a dear friend. He suffered from chronic back pain. He had worked for FedEx and a large box had fallen on him, trapping him under it. The damage that this did to his back caused severe pain for the rest of his life. He eventually had to go on disability. He loved church and loved being reminded that God loved him, even though he was gay. He had been teased all of his life. He grew up in a small town in rural Tennessee. He referred to his Dad as the "John Wayne" type who was tough and serious. It was obvious that, though his Dad was a no nonsense kind of father; he loved his son.

He paid for him to go to a private high school because he was being teased at the public high school. He bought his son a brand new red Midget convertible for his high school graduation. This man's name was Billy Ray Baker. He always went by his first and middle names. Billy Ray was a country boy who happened to be gay. He never attended college. He was very smart. He had a wicked sense of humor. He had a southern drawl about as thick as molasses in the refrigerator. He always called me, "Rev. Looper." He would tell some of the funniest stories about his family. And, then he would say, "Rev. Looper, my family's as crazy as shit house rats!" I would fall out laughing. I could just see some of his family members, even though I had never met them.

Billy Ray had constant health issues. Because of the very strong pain medications he took, he would start having serious side effects and have to be hospitalized. In addition, he suffered from severe depression and was under the care of a psychiatrist. He knew his psychiatrist on a first name basis. When he was in a particularly difficult place emotionally, he would just go to the local psych hospital and check himself in. He would call me and say, "Rev. Looper, this is Billy Ray. I'm back in the nut house getting a tune up." He would give me his code so that I could come visit him. I think Billy Ray and I bonded because my Dad had chronic pain and serious health issues. Billy Ray knew that I understood some of the issues that he faced and I did not judge him. I just tried to meet him where he was.

2008 was a challenge for Billy Ray. His Dad had a stroke, which was devastating for him. He had always seen his Dad as the strong man that he was. Seeing him not able to feed himself and walk was very difficult. Billy Ray also had to have some of his pain meds and psych meds changed. Anytime he had med changes, it took about three months for him to make adjustments. And, that was if there were no interactions. Sometimes he would have the changes and have to go off of the new meds almost as quickly as he had begun them. Managing his meds was a roller coaster emotionally and otherwise for him.

In November of 2008, he called to let me know that he had been admitted to Vanderbilt. He was passing out and the doctors weren't sure why. So, they admitted him for testing. They discovered that one of his new meds was making his blood pressure drop very low. So, he left the hospital on some new medications. Billy Ray was not one to miss church very often. The Sunday following his hospital stay, he came to church. He had a unique gait that I could recognize from far away. The sun was shining down the hall in my eyes as he walked toward the sanctuary. But, I could tell by the gait that Billy Ray had made it to church.

I gave him a big hug and told him that we had missed him. He gave me a kiss on the cheek as he always did and said, "Rev. Looper, you know that I love you, right?" I said, "Billy Ray, yes, I know that you do and I hope you know that I love you as well." He said, "Well, you know I'm a little crazy, but I'm still a good person." I said, "Billy Ray, you are a beautiful child of God! And, I'm so thankful that you are in our church family…crazy and all! Remember, we all got a little crazy inside!" He laughed and entered the sanctuary to his regular seat. He always brought his Bible and he had a genuine love for God. His faith was simple and child-like. There were times when he reminded me that my faith needed to be simple and child-like as well.

I did not know that this would be the last time I would see Billy Ray. The following week, the beginning of December, I received a call from a man named Glen, who helped me with visitation. He had not heard from Billy Ray, who usually called him daily. He decided to go to his apartment. He knocked on the door. Billy Ray's car was in the parking lot. He asked the manager to let him in the apartment. He found Billy Ray lying by his bed face down. He was dead. He called me and I came right over.

It was from here that Glen and I got to experience Billy Ray's family in action. And, sure enough, they were crazy as shit house rats! His three brothers came to the apartment together. Billy Ray lived in Nashville, but his family still lived in the little town he had grown up in. It took them awhile to arrive. The coroner had already come and pronounced Billy Ray dead and the mortuary had picked up his body before his three brothers arrived. If you've seen the movie, Dumb and Dumber... or if you remember the sitcom with the character who would say, "This is my brother, Darrell, and this is my other brother, Darrell," you have a small glimpse of the shit house crazy I'm talking about.

They show up and one of them came with plenty of "nerve pills" 'cause this was just too much to deal with. His name was Butcher Ray Baker. He's the second son. He started going through Billy Ray's medicine cabinet calling out the names of all the meds. One of the other brothers (Boner Ray Baker) started quoting the street value of the prescription drugs in their little town. They thought they had struck gold! Then, the oldest brother started looking for Billy Ray's "papers." We eventually learned that he was referring to his life insurance policies.

They were walking through his little apartment debating on whether to tell their Dad about Billy Ray. They decided that other family members would leak the information, so they needed to tell him. Billy Ray's oldest brother started dialing numbers of relatives.

He would say, "Hey, is this Betty? Betty, this is Bobby Ray. Billy's died!"

That was it. "Billy's died." No words of preparation—just "Billy's died!"

It was all Glen and I could do to keep a straight face as we sat with this family. On one particular call, the phone rang a long time before it was answered. Bobby Ray proceeds to explain that their Dad had a stroke and had to roll his wheel chair over to the phone in order to answer it. I'm thinking, "Oh, my gosh, they are calling their elderly father who has had a stroke to tell him that his youngest son has died?" But before I could say anything, his father answered, "Hello?"

Bobby Ray said, "Diddy, this is Bobby Ray. Billy's died!"

In that moment, I didn't know whether to start crying or burst out laughing. Billy Ray was not kidding when he said his family was "crazy as shit house rats." And, the crazy only got crazier when the wives of Billy Ray's three brothers showed up. Bobby Ray's wife had hair teased to heaven and chain smoked Marlboro Lights. She was a rather large woman who had long fingernails with dirt under them.

The second wife (married to Butcher Ray) was about the size of a tooth pick. She had her nose pierced, had chewed her fingernails down to the quick, and cussed like a sailor. Bobby Ray reminded her several times that Billy Ray's "preacher is sittin' right t'ar."

I just smiled and said, "I know this is a difficult time for all of you."

She, like her husband, was especially interested in Billy Ray's medicine cabinet.

Then, there was Boner Ray's wife. I think she had three teeth in front. But that did not keep her from smiling—or crying—and saying over and over "Por ole Billy Ray. I'm gonna miss him."

To which Boner Ray replied, "Ah, hell, Wilmer, you never wanted to come see him."

To which she lovingly replied, "Boner Ray, shut the f----up before I kick yo ass." The wives of the brothers continued walking through the little apartment divvying up the furniture. The man has just died and his family is dividing up his possessions before he's even buried. Yep, this was definitely some shit house crazy right here.

Glen helped me with Billy Ray's funeral. As crazy as his family was, I wanted him to be remembered in an honorable way. He was, by far, the sane one in the family. Billy Ray told me once what his favorite hymns were; so I suggested to his brothers that we use them.

Of course, Bobby Ray says, "My wife, Willie Maude, really likes *Go Rest High Up on That Mountain* by Vince Gill." Glen and I looked at each other and Glen asked Bobby Ray if he thought we should pick hymns and songs that Billy Ray liked. He says, "Well, yeah, but Willie Maude told me to make sure we played that song." And, you guessed it, we played it!

As I looked at Billy Ray in his casket, he had a slight grin on his face. It was almost like he was saying, "Rev. Looper, I told you my family is crazy as shit house rats. I bet you believe me now."

The fact is, when I think of Billy Ray, I am reminded that we all have a little bit of crazy in us …and we all have family members that are clearly diagnosable. We, the human family, come in all shapes, sizes, colors, abilities and other varying factors that make us diverse.

I loved this man and the laughter we shared. I know when I get to heaven, he will be there to greet me and say, "You didn't believe me! But, I told you, they are crazy as shit house rats!"

CHAPTER 26

Some Losses Are Good

It has now been five years since my surgery. I have lost seventy-six pounds and have been off all my meds for 5 years. I no longer have high blood pressure, diabetes, or sleep apnea. I feel in control of this part of my life. I never realized what carrying around an extra seventy-six pounds was doing to me physically, emotionally, or spiritually. I knew how I felt when I looked in the mirror being so many pounds overweight. I felt shame over my obese body. What I didn't realize was how differently people treated me when I was overweight compared to how I was treated when I lost the weight. It wasn't until I lost the weight and had people respond so positively to me that I understood the negative societal views of obesity. Plain and simple, you are not treated as well when you are overweight. Going through with the surgery was a huge step of faith for me. I was fearful of having an elective surgery. I was fearful of dying on the operating table. I was fearful that the surgery would not work for me. Stepping into the unknowns of this surgery strengthened me in ways I could have not known when I entered the hospital.

I realize today that the extra seventy-six pounds held me in a kind of physical, emotional, and spiritual prison. Losing the weight and keeping it off has greatly increased my self-confidence. My body is lighter and I am able to move more freely. I remember the simple joy of crossing my legs for the first time in years! I like what I see in the mirror looking back at me. Granted, I still occasionally struggle with wrinkles and aging, but the ability to be in a healthier place is wonderful! Sometimes people considering weight loss surgery ask me about my experience. I let them know that it is a personal decision, but I would recommend it to those who feel their weight issues are out of control. Some make judgments, saying things like, "That's the easy way out." And to them I say, it is far from an easy route. The surgery is one day, but the discipline required to remain healthy must be practiced daily for the rest of your life.

One area that I did not expect the surgery to affect was my spiritual walk. Going forward with this surgery was a huge step of faith. I had done all my homework and research on the subject. I had talked to others who'd had the surgery. I had a lengthy conversation with the surgeon to make sure I wouldn't end up anorexic. As I said, it took me two years to decide to have this surgery. Seeing myself with the same health issues as my dad and knowing the quality of life he'd had was a big motivator for me. But the defining moment was when I entered the hospital and actually went forward with it. Never in a million years would I have envisioned myself having such a surgery when I was twenty or thirty. Going through the surgery and having wonderful success has made me less afraid of what may lie in my future.

Going through the surgery, as frightening as it was, has allowed me to face one of my greatest fears—failure. What I have realized is that my fear of failure and the unknown was keeping me from taking risks, personally and as a pastor. I was afraid to think of growing the church and pastoring a congregation of more than 700 people. I was afraid to open my mind to the fact that there could be truth outside my Christian faith. I was afraid to embrace my feminine side because it felt weak. The reality is that life is full of risks. And once we have done our homework by educating ourselves on the issues and addressing the potential risks head on, there comes a time when we have to simply step out in faith, knowing we have done our part and trusting that God will do what we cannot do.

I lost far more than seventy-six pounds following my surgery. I lost much of my fear and anxiety for my future. I gained new physical, emotional, and spiritual space in which I could become a more effective minister and disciple of Christ. I gained new space emotionally to love people and understand the fears that may be trapping them in a prison of self-doubt. I received more room spiritually to allow God's Spirit to dwell in and speak to and through me.

If you would have told me in 2006 that I would be having gastric bypass surgery in 2010, I would have laughed in your face. I can't help but believe that being part of the United Church of Christ opened my mind and heart to new and different things for me and for our church. It taught me—and continues to teach me—that the Still Speaking God that we serve is constantly at work renewing us as individuals and renewing the Church of Jesus Christ. Thanks be to God!

Rev. Cyd Andrews-Looper

CHAPTER 27

Needing Time Off

From 2007 to May of 2011, I faced the deaths of four church members with whom I was very close, as well as my father and my partner's father. In addition, I was pastoring a church that was growing rapidly. I was preaching three sermons each Sunday and attempting to keep up with the pastoral care needs of the congregation. I was one pastor being stretched very thin. The demands on my time and emotions were great.

As the founding pastor of Holy Trinity, I saw this church as my child. I had birthed it and was willing to do whatever it took to make sure it was as healthy as possible and growing. From the time we purchased the property in 2006, the congregation grew faster than we ever imagined. The stress of pastoring a rapidly growing congregation, along with the deaths I had experienced, began taking an emotional toll on me. There was a growing weight that I carried in my mind and spirit. Certainly, God was present and gave me what I needed to face each new challenge. But, the reality of my exhaustion was becoming more and more evident.

As we began 2011, Leigh and I were having some serious problems in our relationship. Looking back, I believe some of it was the collective stress of losing our fathers in 2010 and managing the challenges of our growing congregation. She was on staff at the church as the Church Administrator. We worked together and lived together. For any couple where this is true, there are challenges. We began going to couple's counseling in hopes of working through some of the issues in which we were struggling.

In the fall of 2011, I sat with the personnel committee and began talking about taking some time off. I had never had a sabbatical in all the years I had pastored the church. We had just kicked off the capital campaign to raise money for the new sanctuary. The collective feeling from the personnel committee was that this was not a good time for me to be out of the pulpit. If this had simply been a church that had called me to pastor, I probably would have pushed harder for some time off. But because I was the founding pastor, I felt very responsible for the well-being and health of this congregation. And, I wanted the capital campaign to be a success. This church was my child and I didn't want to do anything that would harm or hinder the good things that were happening. The stresses of church and the struggles in my relationship were very real. However, as a pastor, I had learned to smile and put on the best face possible. It is part of living in the fishbowl of ministry. So, I set my eyes on what was best for the church and tried to ignore the heaviness that I sometimes felt.

CHAPTER 28

On Your Mark, Get Set ...

We kicked off the capital campaign for the new sanctuary during Homecoming, October 2011. We called it ... IMAGINE ...a Hope and a Future! On many occasions, the congregation had heard me reference my life verse, Jeremiah 29:11:

"For I know the plans I have for you declares the Lord. Plans to prosper you and not to harm you. Plans to give you hope and a future."

That verse had resonated with this congregation on many occasions. I do believe that God has plans for us as individuals and as organizations and, I do believe that God's desire is to bless us and not harm us. I believe that, even bad or difficult things that happen to us...God is able, if we give it to Him, to bring about good and blessings from our pain and loss. The key is keeping ourselves focused on God and giving whatever we are facing to Him.

The fall of 2011 was truly an exciting time. It had taken us almost a year to prepare the congregation to step into this campaign. And, if I'm honest, I had a level of anxiety over it. My anxiety did not come from my relationship with God; but, rather, a fear that the congregation would not respond effectively. We paid a campaign consultant $67,000 to guide us. We knew there was no way we could raise nearly 2 million dollars on our own. We needed help in how to run an effective campaign. We had some folks leave the church when we moved forward with the campaign. I talked with them but, in the end, I had to lovingly let them go. You see, as a pastor, not everyone can make the journey with you. Sometimes, they simply aren't emotionally or spiritually prepared for the change that moving forward means.

It does not mean in any form or fashion that they are "bad people" or "negative people." It means that this is not the journey that God has for them. Those who are supposed to make the journey will stay and participate in making the move forward. I think as a young pastor, I thought everyone in the church needed to be on board before we could move forward but, over the years, I learned that, sometimes people are simply not ready or equipped to make the journey. The last thing you need to do is give into their wishes...or judge them. Acknowledge their concerns or fears. But, explain that God is leading—and you and the congregation must be obedient. Pray with these individuals and let them know that you love them. Then, lovingly put them in God's hands. God will take care of them. It is important that you not spend your time moving forward with trying to coax these individuals along. In the end, they will either join you or they won't. You must spend your energy seeking God and leading your congregation to fulfill the ministry and vision that God is calling you to.

The Vestry asked my partner, Leigh, who was serving as the Church Administrator at this time, to manage and coordinate the capital campaign and the build that would follow. I honestly don't know what we would have done if she had not been on staff. No one else on staff had the organizational skills that she possessed. Leigh was a perfect fit to coordinate the capital campaign and manage the build.

We had three possible levels to the campaign. The lowest amount was based on simply building a new sanctuary. The second included a van to transport individuals who would have to park offsite and some other upgrades. The third included purchasing the house and lot behind the church and building additional parking.

Obviously, we hoped we could reach the 2.5 million of the third level so we could build additional parking. However, I was going to be pleased if we reached the first level. This was our first capital campaign. It takes an enormous amount of human resources to pull off a successful campaign and it requires serious commitment from the members of the church. You are asking them to give significantly above and beyond their regular tithes and offerings. They have to see the vision and be inspired to do their part. As pastor, you first have to clearly see the vision and have a deep conviction that this must happen. If you lack focus or conviction, your congregation will know it and not follow you. Your conviction and faith will keep you optimistic when folks start to worry about the results as you are moving forward and they will talk to each other. In the end, however, they are looking to you to inspire them and lead them forward. So, you need to be prayed up and put your "big girl panties" on before you launch any major giving campaign in your church or organization.

The capital campaign ran through the following June of 2012. What a worship celebration we had when we announced that we had raised 1.8 million dollars! At the end of service, we had a congregational meeting and voted to move forward with building the new sanctuary. In October, at our 16th Homecoming Anniversary, we broke ground and blessed the space on which our new sanctuary would be built.

As I took that scoop of earth in my shovel, tears came to my eyes as I thought about how far we had come. In that moment,

Rev. Cyd Andrews-Looper

I was envisioning that little Bible study group back in 1996. NEVER in a million years would I or they have thought our efforts would become this amazing and vibrant church body. As I tossed the earth to the side and said the prayer of blessing, my heart was about to burst with thanksgiving to God. How incredibly faithful God is when we simply do our part and give the rest to Him. I had seen this over and over in my faith walk and now, once again, I was experiencing the faithfulness of God with my brothers & sisters at Holy Trinity. I believe all of our faith journeys were strengthened that day. The ground on which we stood felt holy. And, the Spirit rising up within our souls was palpable. There is no greater experience on this earth than partnering with God to build the kingdom!

CHAPTER 29

Back in the Closet

In the late winter of 2012, Leigh and I had decided that our ability to be in a romantic relationship was lost. We had been to counseling and tried our best to find new connections but nothing seemed to bring what we both wanted and needed. We met with the personnel committee, let them know that our relationship was ending, and we wanted to make an announcement to the congregation.

There was an obvious shock to the members of the personnel committee. There were tears as we explained that we had been struggling to find meaningful and life-giving connections since 2011. We had love and respect for each other but our ability to connect romantically was gone and to try to force something that was not there was bringing more harm to both of us. Our working relationship at the church was excellent. As a matter of fact, our working partnership had strengthened once we took the pressure of being in a romantic relationship off the table.

As we talked through our desire to share this information with the congregation, the collective concern of the personnel committee was that we were still in the midst of the capital campaign. This announcement would hit the congregation hard and affect the outcome of the campaign. Knowing that the building campaign would follow the capital campaign, they felt that the earliest we could share this information was in early to the mid-2014.

As I have said earlier, if this had been simply a church who had called me to pastor, I probably would have refused to bear the emotional weight that they were suggesting. But, I was the founding pastor and was willing to do what was going to be best for this church I had birthed.

So, Leigh and I basically "went into the closet" by living as roommates. We moved into separate bedrooms and tried to make the most of a difficult situation. We both longed to find love and happiness again but we loved this church and felt we needed to listen to the concerns of the personnel committee. Obviously, it was important that we maintain appearances while we were at church. We had to be careful not to reference "my bedroom" or "my bathroom." And, the shared respect we had for each other certainly grew in those moments. We poured ourselves more deeply into the church.

What began to grow between us was a friendship. We were able to honestly share about what we wanted and needed in a life partner. We would talk about women that we found attractive and, when we would become frustrated with the situation in which we found ourselves, we would try to remember that we were doing it for this congregation that we loved so dearly.

I will say that there is something very unhealthy about this kind of arrangement. We knew and understood why we had been asked to do it. But, in the same way that we had been closeted in our past concerning our sexual orientation, we were now living closeted lives again. The inability to be honest eats away at parts of you like emotional cancer. Your longing to be honest and to pursue what will bring you happiness is not an option. And, in the same way many of us resented our families when we were in the closet, I think Leigh and I had some resentment over this weight we were carrying. I think our sanity came from being so busy that we seldom had time to really think or feel it deeply. We did our best to maintain appearances and be happy with circumstances that seemed beyond our control.

Rev. Cyd Andrews-Looper

CHAPTER 30

Hiring Another Minister

In the proposed 2012 budget, there was a position for another full time minister. I was thrilled that the Finance Committee and the Vestry heard my need for help. I asked not to be given a raise so that we could use any additional monies to hire another staff person. We took our time in the search and interview process. We knew that we needed someone who would be a perfect fit for our unique congregation. I felt strongly that we needed to hire a man. And, given that 85-90% of our congregation came from evangelical churches (Baptist, Pentecostal, and Church of Christ), we needed someone who understood the spiritual dynamics of these traditions. In our search process, we initially narrowed the choice down to two candidates. However, as we talked through the needs of the congregation, we really felt that neither of them was really the perfect candidate for this new position.

One of the personnel committee members said she had a friend—a former Southern Baptist who had worked in youth camps. He was living in New York City with his partner and no longer in ministry. She reached out to him via Facebook and he expressed a strong interest in talking to us.

Our first interview with him was via Skype. We liked his energy, his spirit, and the answers he gave to some of our challenging questions. After the interview we were very excited and began to seriously consider what it would mean to offer him this position. We decided to fly him and his partner down to Nashville for a weekend. We again sat with him and asked him more challenging questions. He also brought questions which, for me, was a good sign. He was obviously interested in joining us in this ministry.

At the end of the worship service, I sat with him and told him that we were very interested in bringing him on staff. I explained that we had gone through the interview process with several candidates and had narrowed it down to two. But, as we talked through things, we felt that neither of them would be the perfect fit we needed. I shared that we all felt that he could step into our church family and connect with the members, become part of the pastoral staff in helping grow our Christian education, and respond to the pastoral care needs.

Bryan Curry moved to Nashville and came on staff in August of 2012. It was one of the best decisions we could have made in building our staff. He was everything that we imagined and more. I loved having a colleague with which to share the pastoral responsibilities and I loved his sense of humor. He brought great energy, fresh ideas and a warm spiritual presence that ministered to our congregation.

The decision to wait and pray before settling on our original candidates was very wise. Not that either of them couldn't have done the job. They were well qualified and good men. But, we knew that there was a perfect fit out there … and because we loved our congregation, it was worth the wait to find him. From my current vantage point, I am especially thankful that Bryan was the person we chose. Somehow God knew what the future would hold and the needs that would arise.

CHAPTER 31

Mud, Mud and More Mud!

In January of 2013, our little piece of property was covered with a number of large yellow machines that proceeded to dig and move enormous amounts of earth. If you have ever been part of building a house or other building, you know that it doesn't start with the bricks and wood. It starts with the moving of dirt everywhere. And, it looks like big boys playing in the dirt with their toys! One day they move dirt in this pile. The next day, they move it to another pile. For someone who has no understanding of the building process, it was quite confusing.

Moving all this dirt around during a Tennessee winter means lots of mud. It doesn't snow much and the weather, most often, consists of overcast, dreary and rainy days. So, the big boys would play with dirt a while, then it would begin to rain and they would have to stop.

The church staff had to contend with more mud than we had ever imagined. Our Administrative Assistant actually lost his shoe as his foot mired up nearly to his knee in the mud. Each week, he changed the message on the church sign. And, the path to the sign was the muddiest. On Saturdays, my partner and I would buy bales of hay and scatter it across the muddy parking lot. We wanted the experience of those attending the church to be as positive as possible in the midst of the build.

Home Depot became very familiar with our faces every Saturday. They knew exactly what we wanted and why!

As we moved into summer, the building actually started taking shape. We could walk inside with our hard hats on and see the progress. Initially, the sanctuary space looked smaller than we imagined. Then, as the carpet was laid and the walls painted, it looked larger than we anticipated. It was so exciting to see this building go up before our very eyes. It was like God was bringing our faith and work into reality. Again, watching the progress was something that built our collective faith as a congregation. And, as the building was going up, we had new people pledge to the campaign. They came to the church and felt the excitement and wanted to be part of this new journey.

As I have stated before, I am very thankful for my partner at the time and the work she did to make sure we had a successful campaign, as well as a successful build. I think some of the men she dealt with thought she was "just a woman" and didn't understand what was going on.

The fact was, they didn't know her. She was educating herself with each new process so that she could speak their language. She knew the right specs for each new stage and she made sure everything was done properly. She did not hesitate to call meetings with the builder to talk about concerns with particular sub-contractors. She instilled a confidence in the congregation that this building was being put together properly and the money they were giving was well worth it.

By the end of summer, the building looked quite complete but there were still dozens of little details that had to be dealt with before we could receive a permit for use. As we moved into September, we decided to delay our Homecoming Celebration because we wanted our first worship service in the new building to be during Homecoming. The level of growing excitement was palpable.

In the 17 years I had pastored this church, there had been many ups and downs. I 'don't think any of us would have envisioned the amazing things that were happening. I believe God was blessing us because we had kept ourselves postured in faith since I went full time in 2005. The Spirit of God is moved by our simply childlike faith and always responds. We were living testimonies of God's faithfulness. When we live in faith and lift our needs to God, God will always meet them.

Rev. Cyd Andrews-Looper

CHAPTER 32

Walking With Those Are Hurting

In September of 2013, I received an odd call from two women in Florida. They told me that the sister of one of our congregants had called them asking them to call me. The woman in our congregation had a very strained relationship with her family, who lived in Ohio. When her son was around 4 or 5, she came out and divorced her husband. Her family, including her parents, proceeded to shun her and keep her from seeing her son. She had moved to Nashville and made friends who became her family.

Her son had grown up not really knowing her. Three years earlier, he and his wife gave birth to a little girl. She was thrilled that he invited her to come and see her granddaughter. But, after that meeting, he did not contact her again. She believed it was most likely because of her mother. For whatever reason, her mother had been intentional about hurting her and shunning her since she came out many years before.

This call I was receiving was to tell me that her son, who was only in his late twenties, had been electrocuted that morning. He was an electrician and was working on a house. He fell off a ladder and landed on a live wire. He was dead as soon as he hit the ground. His aunt knew two woman in Florida who were friends of his mother's (I think one of them may have grown up with them in Ohio) and they just happened to have her phone number. These women were calling me asking me to please go to this woman's work and share this news with her.

I had known this woman for several years but I did not know the extent to which she had been shunned by her family. I did not even know that she had a son. As a mother myself, my heart ached at the thought of sharing this tragic news with her.

I found out her place of employment and called her boss. I let him know the news. He was more aware of her family situation and he was very concerned for her. I told him I was on my way to meet with her and share this news. He went to two of her co-workers with whom she was good friends and let them know that I was on my way.

When I arrived, he met me at the front door and then called her co-workers back to his office. I shared with them what I knew. She had obviously gotten close to them. They knew more details about her family situation.

Her boss then went to bring her to his office. She walked in slowly. As soon as she saw me, she said, "What is wrong?" I asked her to sit while I knelt beside her and began telling her the news I had received. As you can imagine, she collapsed into my arms. Her co-workers surrounded her and held her, crying along with her. Her boss let her know she could take off whatever time she needed. She had been doing an intake and asked one of her co-workers to complete it. Then she gathered her coat and purse. Fortunately, I had asked someone to drive me to her place of work.

So, I drove her car to her home while the other person followed us. This woman, as you can imagine, was numb. She would say random thoughts that came into her mind about her son. That he had the bluest eyes. That he had large feet. That she had never really had a relationship with him because her family kept her from him. "But," she said, "He knows and understands everything now. He knows how much I loved him and how I longed to be in his life. He knows that all that they told him were lies." She cried as she shared this awareness.

We arrived at her home and saw that there were already three cars in the driveway. The friends from Florida had obviously called other friends who were close to her to make sure she would not be alone in these moments. I spoke with her sister and let her know that she was doing ok. Her sister gave the account of the past more than 20 years—of how their mother became extremely hateful and vindictive toward her sister. How their mother made sure that her sister never saw her son. How their mother would "punish" other family members if they had any contact with this woman. It was incredibly sad that a family would allow one individual to control the relationships of the other family members. But, this woman's mother had controlled her daughters, her husband, her grandson and granddaughter in law and now, her great granddaughter. She had done everything she could to make sure her grandson believed that his mother had abandoned him when he was very young. She had made sure that he and every other family member shunned her. There was a hate that this mother lived out that was unbelievable. I honestly don't know how any human being can hate someone else so much that they will go to these lengths to hurt them but here was living proof that this level of hate existed.

The next day, this woman received word from her sister that she was not welcome at the funeral. They were denying her the opportunity to say goodbye to her only child whom they had kept from her most of his life. She was beyond broken.

I called her sister and tried to reason with her but it was obvious that their mother had serious control over the whole family. I called the mortuary and asked if this woman could have a private viewing of her son. They said "yes." She found someone to drive her there and she was able to spend some time alone saying goodbye to her only child. The pain that I saw in her eyes in the months to come was obvious. Sometimes after service she would fall into my arms bawling her eyes out at the loss of her son and the incredible pain that she carried because she'd never been allowed to have a relationship with him.

She is one of the most deeply spiritual people that I know. As she moved through 2014, I watched her gain strength and hope again. Her son has visited her in dreams and she has found great comfort from that. Her friends are still like her family.

For those who have been shunned by a birth family, you know the power and place of your "chosen family." They are the people with whom you celebrate. They are the people with whom you mourn. They love you and walk with you through life. I am thankful for how those in the LGBTQ community form their chosen family units. There is a closeness and strength that cannot be broken. And, the closeness and strength is borne out of pain and loss. I believe our chosen families share the purest of love for us in this world. The love is not based on blood; but, on a shared understanding of being different and being shunned by some because of that difference. There is almost a "tribal mentality" that forms among chosen families. Nothing will keep them from being present for each other for their loving connections have been forged through pain. I am personally thankful for my "chosen family" and "tribe." It is small; but, it is incredibly strong and daily reminds me of the deep love found in the heart of God!

CHAPTER 33

It Doesn't Get Any Better Than This!

On November 17th, 2013, we had our first worship service in our new sanctuary. I can't even begin to tell you how electric the atmosphere was. The sanctuary was designed to seat nearly 500 people but the final count was well over 600 individuals in attendance, with many standing in the lobby during service.

Our United Church of Christ Conference Minister, as well as a number of members of Brookmeade Congregational were our special guests. The members of Brookmeade had loved us and given us a safe space to worship in 1999 when no one else would. In many ways, they saw us as an extension of their ministry. Their presence and support that day meant the world to me.

Randy Craft, our Music Director, and his assistant, Cameron Cleland, prepared absolutely amazing music. The choir was full and their energy was magnetic. It was like heaven came down and touched us.

While I don't like to brag on myself very often, I believe the sermon I delivered was inspired by God's Spirit. I used this Homecoming Sunday to begin a new sermon series entitled, **We Are Not Ashamed**. I reminded all of us that when we claim our identity as children of God, there is no shame. And, our ministry and mission at Holy Trinity was to proclaim and live out this good news. With our new sanctuary, we were going to be able to welcome hundreds of new souls who needed to be reminded of their worth as children of God.

Our parking attendants, ushers, and greeters were doing an amazing job making sure our guests felt loved and welcomed. When the staff members looked into each other's eyes, there was a shared knowledge that we were part of something beyond the earthly realm. This was the work of God and we were part of kingdom-building.

Instead of our usual potluck, we had food trucks lined up in the parking lot. Bruce Barnes, a man who has an amazing spiritual gift of hospitality, was present and made sure that all the bases were covered. He had decorated the church and tables beautifully. When Bruce decorates, it is more than mere trimming. He has a way of putting his soul into it. To sit at a table he has decorated is to feel blessed. There is a warmth and love that comes with the experience.

Looking back over my eighteen years as pastor of this church, this service and this celebration was truly the highlight of my ministry. I can't imagine experiencing that kind of spiritual and emotional high again in my ministry. I'm so thankful that God honored me by allowing me to lead His church to this place of celebration. It was a little taste of heaven on earth!

CHAPTER 34

Time for a Raise?

In the September prior to our Homecoming Celebration, I knew the Finance Committee had started to prepare the proposed 2014 budget. I had passed up a raise in years past because it was more important to me that we hire additional staff. The congregation was growing and their needs were far greater than I could handle.

But in the fall of 2013 I was tired and frazzled. I had a feeling that my salary was well below the average salary for other United Church of Christ ministers in the South who had my education, years of experience, and who were pastoring churches the size of Holy Trinity. I called the eleven conferences in the South and spoke with the conference ministers. What I discovered was the salary range among the 11 conferences for pastors with my education, experience, and who were leading churches the size of Holy Trinity was $70,000-$120,000.

I asked the church committees to increase my salary so that it fell within this range and, after a painful negotiation, my salary was increased but not to the extent I felt was appropriate particularly considering my lack of vacations or sabbaticals.

It can be a real challenge as a pastor when you have to trust your leadership to represent your needs and intentions to those making decisions. But, you really have no choice. Your life and your livelihood are in the hands of those who make the financial decisions. I believe most members of the Vestry—and any governing body—have compassion and care for the spiritual leader(s) of their congregation. However, when the person or persons responsible for communicating your requests and needs is burned out or dealing with stress within their own lives, often what is communicated may not be accurate or complete in the details.

Looking back, that negative interaction seemed to set a tone for 2014.

CHAPTER 35

"Lovingly Releasing Each Other"

As we entered 2014, as much as I wanted to, I didn't possess the excitement which I usually have at the beginning of a new year. My partner, Leigh, who had worked many, many long hours in the prior two years, asked for 40 days off for rest and renewal. And, if anyone deserved it, she did. I was glad that she was granted this time off. However, I had been wanting and needing time away since 2011. Consistently, the collective thought of the personnel committee was that the congregation could not handle my being out of the pulpit for a month or more. But, I found myself feeling overwhelmingly exhausted and emotionally disconnected. And, there was a growing resentment inside me that I had been expected to grit my teeth and simply keep going.

Her time away was a turning point for both of us. We were away from each other and able to have our own space to think, feel and exist freely and safely. When she returned the beginning of March, we sat and talked. We shared with each other how much we loved our time alone. We also realized in our times of solitude that we could not go on living as roommates. We had a love and respect for each other...and we both wanted the other to be happy. We each wanted the freedom to move on and find love and happiness. We decided that it was time to "come out of the closet" and share this information with the congregation.

We met with the Personnel Committee and shared with them our desire. I met with the Conference Minister and shared this news. She agreed to come to Nashville on the Sunday we made the announcement. The plan we had seemed well thought out. The Personnel Committee felt that we simply needed to say that we were "lovingly releasing each other" and maintain this consistent message when questions were asked.

However, what I knew was that we had been living together as roommates for about two years. I knew that we were well past the angry stage. I knew that we both were ready to move on and start dating. Not to jump into a serious relationship, but to simply date and feel alive again inside. I didn't feel that simply saying we are "lovingly releasing each other" was going to bode well with members of the church who didn't understand some of the history of our relationship.

It is in moments like this where living in the fish bowl of ministry can be a tremendous challenge. You find yourself asking…"what does the congregation need to know?"…"where is the line between my private life and them understanding a complicated situation?"…"how do I avoid assumptions and gossip?"

Having lived in the fish bowl for eighteen years, I knew the congregation needed some background of our relationship. I knew we would both most likely be dating and I knew if we only said, "we are lovingly releasing each other," the congregation would assume that the breakup had just happened. They would not understand where we were emotionally. They would not understand that we were relieved and happy to be "out of the closet" and free to move forward separately.

Leigh is a very private person and she insisted that we simply say that we were lovingly releasing each other. She felt that our private lives were not the business of the congregation. So, on Sunday, May 4, 2014, following the worship service, we made the announcement that we were "lovingly releasing each other." In my remarks, I tried to give some bits of history and explain that we had been living as roommates and friends for nearly two years. I'm not sure that any of this was really heard. The congregation was hit hard by the news.

I'm not sure Leigh or I realized how the congregation saw our partnership. Somehow, our twelve-year relationship and our partnership in ministry at the church brought a level of stability for many in the congregation. To say that we were the pillars would be an understatement.

Looking back, I had no idea just how emotionally and mentally burned out I was going into 2014. I believe I was able to function because I had a very predictable weekly routine. As long as that routine was in place, I could operate without much thought or emotion. The significant changes that happened following the announcement began to disrupt this routine. All of a sudden, I was having to think and feel outside what was familiar.

If I had it to do all over again, I would have identified a group of friends who could walk with me and advise me on this uncharted journey. The reality was, I was dating someone who made me feel the way I had longed to feel for years. She made me feel beautiful again. I had pretty much given up hope of ever really feeling attractive again. At 51, following weight loss surgery, having an AARP membership, and stepping into the world of sagging skin, let's just say this girl had given up on catching anyone's eye again. But, thankfully, I was wrong!

Within the first month of the announcement, Leigh and I both began dating other people. It felt good to feel alive again and have a romantic connection in my life. However, I honestly was too burned-out emotionally to have a healthy perspective on how my dating would affect the congregation. And, in my burned-out state, along with some underlying resentment for all that I had given up for the congregation, part of me was too tired to care. I simply wanted to live my life and be happy. I was tired of having to live my life for what was best for the congregation without any time away for rest or renewal. In that place, I made some decisions that I will forever regret.

Probably the biggest regret was choosing to sit with Angie, the woman I was dating, for the gospel sing that happened quarterly. I was not preaching, so I chose to sit with her and she put her arm around me. At the end of service, we had communion and we went forward to receive communion together. Again, in my burned-out oblivious state, I had no clue how this looked or would affect the congregation.

In the week that followed, I received a couple of emails. One in particular was scathing. First, the person asked how I could disrespect Leigh by sitting with the woman I was dating in service. What he or others did not know was that Leigh was also dating someone...and the woman was singing in the choir; otherwise, they might have sat together in that service as well.

He also wanted to know how in the world I could be dating someone so soon after breaking up. I responded to his email and tried explain that I wasn't disrespecting Leigh. That she was in fact also dating someone. I also tried to explain that she and I had been living as roommates for almost two years. We were well past the anger and resentment stage of a breakup. We, in fact, were good friends. And, when we made the announcement, we both were ready to move forward and start dating if the opportunity presented itself.

I've learned something since 2014...it is best to sit with some individuals in person and talk through these kinds of concerns instead of responding via email or text. You see, when you write something, it is there and can be shared with anyone.

It can be misinterpreted and shared in ways that you never intended. And, that is exactly what happened with my email interaction with this person. It ended up on Facebook!!! You can imagine what happened from there.

Individuals, some whom I didn't even know, began to comment and question my integrity and motives. One of the first comments made was, "Who starts dating so soon after a breakup? I think she was having an affair."

From there, other questions began to fly, "So if they've been lying to us about their relationship for two years, what else are they lying about?" (they did not know that we had been told by the personnel committee in 2012 that it was best that we "go in the closet" until a better time to tell the truth).

Then, the same person asked, "If they are lying about their relationship, what else are they lying about? You know they are behind in the budget? Maybe they are lying about the money as well."

From here, an individual who volunteered at the church chimed in on the Facebook debacle. Leigh would sometimes ask this person to reconcile the credit card statements with the receipts. His response was, "well, as a matter of fact, I could not believe how much money Pastor Cindy spends on meals…and she seldom has her receipts." He then shares a receipt from the month prior from a restaurant across the street from the church for approximately $140.

What he did not know was that on that date, I had invited the leadership of a small church west of Nashville to spend a Saturday with me and Leigh. I was helping them affiliate with the UCC and helping them find a pastor. After our meeting I took all of us (about 11 people) to this restaurant for dinner. The assumption this man made was that I had spent this amount on a meal for Leigh and friends.

Sadly, when this kind of fodder is being discussed in a public forum like Facebook, there is little you can do to defend yourself. I tried to respond to the accusations coming in, but was simply met with more attacks. To this day, there are individuals who took comments made in that Facebook feed as fact and believe that I cheated on Leigh, believe that I never had receipts for expenses, believe I spent large amounts on personal meals, and believe that I took money from the church. None of these comments were true then, nor are they true now.

As I stated earlier, I was in no shape emotionally or mentally to deal with these kinds of attacks. I began clinging tightly to Angie, the woman I was dating, but in many ways was beginning to unravel emotionally. Nothing about my former safe routine was present. I was being attacked at every corner. I began to question whom I could trust. I wasn't even sure I could trust Leigh. The weight of the burnout from years prior, along with the attacks and stress, was more than I could manage.

What I needed in those moments was for the personnel committee and Vestry members to sit with me and say, "Things have gotten out of hand. There's a lot of gossip and drama going on. Pastor Cindy, what do you need right now? Let's figure out a plan that will help you find some rest and let's talk to the congregation about how we all need to be responding in these moments. Together, let's figure this out as a church family." That is what I needed most.

However, that is not what happened.

CHAPTER 36

Things Begin Unraveling

Yes, what I needed was for all that was happening to be handled within the parameters of our Holy Trinity family. However, some individuals in leadership chose to contact the UCC (United Church of Christ) Conference Minister and ask them to come in and oversee the drama that had unfolded following my sitting with Angie in service and the email which ended up on Facebook.

I was blind-sided in a surprise meeting in July 2014. The Vestry chair changed the usual meeting from Sunday to mid-week and asked me to grill hamburgers for everyone. I walked into a meeting in which there were only 3 individuals around the table who knew why the meeting was occurring and why there were UCC individuals present from Atlanta and Pleasant Hill. The other six Vestry members and staff members were all as clueless as I was. Two Vestry members and one personnel committee member knew why the meeting was actually happening. When I was the last one to arrive to the meeting because I had been grilling hamburgers for everyone, I then found out the reason for the meeting. It was to confront me on the issues related to my dating Angie and the rumors and drama that had arisen from the email ending up on Facebook. It was to confront me on my lack of awareness.

Looking back, it is too bad that there wasn't more awareness concerning how burned-out I was in 2014…and just how raw and traumatizing it was to be blindsided by church leadership in this surprise meeting. Unfortunately, not all of those on the personnel committee knew just how burned-out I was in those moments. There were really very few individuals around the table who knew. They had walked with me…and with Leigh for several years. Perhaps they were, as individuals, facing their own challenges. Looking back at the events that began in July 2014, the greatest pain comes from those who I thought loved me and had my back. They knew more than anyone in the congregation just how burned-out I was when that meeting occurred. To sit in a meeting and be confronted in that manner without any means of preparation or prior knowledge is difficult when you're in great emotional health. However, to be treated and handled in this manner when you are in a burned-out and compromised emotional state seems cruel and punitive. For me, the shock and pain of it all was simply too much. I had to walk out. I have no idea what was said, thought or assumed in my absence.

One of the Vestry members who was and is a dear friend, and who had also been blindsided by this meeting came out to talk to me. She said, "Cindy, I don't like what they are saying or implying. You are not in there to defend yourself. And, I truly question the motives of our church leadership and am unsure of how well this UCC team will handle you or this church. You have got to come in and show them your strength. You've got to show them what they are obviously blind to at the moment. I don't like the direction the conversation has gone already. They want you to take time off— which you definitely need—but they are insisting that you have no contact with anyone in the church. I know you have little or no family support. I know this church is your family. I can't support what they want to do unless you are part of the decision. Please come in and talk."

I came back into the meeting and tried to muster something deep inside me. I shared how God had led me to start a Bible study and how it had grown into what we knew and loved as Holy Trinity Nashville.

When a member of the UCC team began to respond, I felt that he had heard nothing I had said. There was a condescension that I felt from him as he implied I was a control freak in my leadership style. Little did he know that I had been conditioned by the primary church leadership to give all I had—my time, my love, my sweat, my tears—for this church. I had been conditioned by not being given a sabbatical, by being asked to live with my former partner as roommates for two years, by begrudgingly being given a raise. It's interesting that he made the comment that "they have been begging you to take off." It was obvious that I had missed a number of opportunities to respond or defend myself in the conversations that happened in my absence. And, I still was in shock over this surprise meeting. At no time did anyone "beg me to take off."

I was told that their recommendation was for me to take a two month non-communicative sabbatical. The thought of having time off was a welcome relief. The non-communicative part seemed punitive. When I tried to explain that having even a handful of individuals with whom I could have contact would be helpful for me. The response was that I needed to create a new support system outside the church. This was a great idea but the UCC team obviously had no idea where I really was emotionally or what I truly needed. They made assumptions and gave direction. At no time did they sit with me and say, "Cindy, you have grown and pastored this church for many years. You are obviously not in a good place. What is going on with you? What do you need in this moment? What would be most helpful to you right now?"

How I wish the UCC team would have cared enough in those moments to sit with me, hear me, and allow me to share where I was and what I was needing. They sat and listened to a group of individuals recount events of the prior month and perhaps months prior to that but there is no way they could have had a truly accurate picture without talking to me. I believe this is the first point in which this UCC team failed me, and ultimately failed this church. There were other points that followed.

Rev. Cyd Andrews-Looper

CHAPTER 37

My Two Month Sabbatical

Angie, the woman whom I was dating, brought me a great deal of comfort in the weeks ahead but I don't think either of us realized the stress this situation was going to put on our brand new relationship. Though we never really talked about it until much later, she had no idea the emotional place I was in when I took the time off. I was really in no emotional state to be dating. One thing for which we both agreed was that she was placed in my life for one specific reason during that season of our lives. She was in my life to give me hope and strength and to keep me alive. Our souls agreed before entering this current physical experience that we would share nine months together. In that time, I would face emotional and mental exhaustion. I would face betrayal. I would face pain and loss that would bring me close to suicide.

Angie's soul agreed to be the one to walk with me in this particular season. The only way I could face the pain and loss and survive was to have someone of strong physical stature who could hold me and make me feel safe. Someone who had strong faith and who could keep my eyes on a God who was bigger than any troubles I was facing. Someone who had mental and emotional tenacity to ride the emotional waves—the highs and lows that characterized my life in this season. I needed someone who would and could walk through the fire with me, knowing they would get burned, in order to keep me alive. Angela Dittrich will someday hear, "Well done, good and faithful servant." Mainly because of the generosity and love with which she lives her life but specifically, in my season, for taking pain and pulling me out of the fire. I am alive today because of this woman; and I will share a bit more details in a later chapter.

During my sabbatical, I began doing some things that brought me peace and rest. I began journaling daily and meditating. Getting my thoughts on paper daily was so helpful and meditating quieted the racing of my mind. I spent one of the two months at the beach. This is one place in which I feel the Presence of God as nowhere else.

I took long walks on the beach. I talked to God. I watched the sun set and rise. My soul was able to "light" and be still in a way it had not in years. There was an inner peace rising up within me. I also began taking pictures of the sunset and the birds on the beach. And, I felt led to buy acrylic paint and canvas. I began painting from this very raw place deep within my soul. God was doing some amazing things within my spirit as I simply rested in my existence as a child of God.

I sat one day and did an entire life review. I looked honestly at my life. I looked at places and events from my past where I had made good decisions and made a difference in people's lives. I also looked at the moments when I seemed to make less than stellar decisions. Consistently, my poor decisions correlated to the times when I was not tending to my emotional, physical, or spiritual health. It was simply a lack of self-care. I wanted to succeed in the eyes of those around me. So, I would simply push myself a little harder, even when my life was pouring over with stress. Self-care did not come natural for me. Somehow, when duty called, I was supposed to be present no matter what. This attitude brought me to burnout on a number of occasions and it affected every romantic relationship of my past. The ability to pull away and not feel guilty was difficult but, if I didn't learn to do this, I was simply going to repeat this same cycle over and over.

I sat and began making a list of things I needed to be doing weekly and monthly to ensure I didn't repeat this unhealthy cycle again. One of the first things was to sit with the Personnel Committee and Vestry and be honest with them about what I needed in order to stay in a healthy place mentally and emotionally. My two days off each week would be intentionally spent away from the church. I was going to ask for one weekend off per month for a year. At that time, we had two additional ministerial staff who could preach. Taking a weekend a month would allow me to write and paint. These are two things that still bring me a great deal of comfort. I looked forward to sitting and talking with the leadership of Holy Trinity. I also looked forward to being back with my church family.

By the fifth and sixth week of my sabbatical, I was wondering what in the world was going on in Nashville. So much of my existence was isolated from those I loved. About two weeks into the sabbatical, I had texted some folks I considered to be my friends when I caught a two-to-three pound catfish in a pond of one of the Vestry members. I received no response. They were taking the non-communicative piece of my sabbatical seriously.

The only regular human contact I had was with Angie. We were still getting to know each other. Not being able to share fun events or funny situations with anyone in my church family began feeling like an emotional limb of my life had been cut off. I was having to experience so much of this time in a void.

Because of the nature of our new dating relationship, the connection and dynamic were not the same as someone who had known me for years and who got my humor.

While I was at the beach, I reached out to some folks and tried to get some sense of what was going on with the process back in Nashville. I was excited about the renewal I was feeling. I felt that the congregation was more than ready for me to be back in the pulpit. We had very well-equipped staffers filling the pulpit. But, they were not the Senior Pastor—seen as the spiritual mother and visionary for the congregation.

I certainly was ready to return to my church family and be back in the pulpit. The responses I received from the few texts I sent were distant and cold. Angie warned me that she believed the UCC and some of the church leadership were monitoring my interactions. The thought of my worth and value being judged and assessed based on my reaching-out and trying to find out what was going in Nashville seemed cruel and punitive. It lacked compassion for another human being and certainly did not represent the UCC which I had come to love.

The reality was that this was exactly what was going on. Many months later I found out that my texts were being read aloud in the Vestry meetings. And, harsh words and judgments were being laid on me without understanding, care, or compassion. Some of the very people I had prayed for and with—people for whom I had walked alongside through breakups and deaths in their families— these people were blind to what it meant to be a brother or sister in Christ to their own pastor. What was blinding them?

I believe it was the fact that they, themselves, were wounded.

You see, we all have wounds. Wounds from childhood. Wounds from junior high and high school. Wounds from how we were treated by parents, teachers, and fellow students. Wounds from how we were treated by former church members and pastors. When we are involved in highly emotional events in which someone's leadership or behavior is being questioned, it is easy for our own wounds to affect how we see the events, and feel the emotions.

We begin to operate in that hurt emotional space and we often find a convenient target on which to unleash our personal pain. I believe I became a convenient target for some on the Vestry. No longer could they see me as the founding pastor of this vibrant church who had invested 18 years of her life; and grown it to a congregation of over 750 unduplicated individuals attending each month. They began to see me as someone who had intentionally hurt them. And, in that place all they could feel or see was how to put me in my place. This was, for many, a perfect opportunity to connect to out their own deep internal wounds and find some level of release from the feelings of anger and revenge that had been pushed down for so many years.

I have found myself wondering if it was this kind of personal woundedness and pride that was ultimately unleashed on Jesus. Those who crucified Him were absolutely blind. I certainly am not Jesus Christ. But, Lent of 2015 resonated in my spirit as it never has in years past. Somehow I found great comfort and understanding in the pain and suffering of Jesus. And, I saw and understood those who crucified Him in a way I had not before. They did not see Him because they were blinded by their personal pain and keeping the rules. There was no grace. Surely, this seems part of our human condition. But, when you are the target for the condemnation, it is hard to understand what you have done to deserve such harsh treatment and punishment. My painful experience of the last year truly brought me closer to Jesus. For that I am indeed thankful.

Rev. Cyd Andrews-Looper

CHAPTER 38

My Return to Nashville

At the beginning of my last week at the beach, a member of the UCC team called me asking if I would return to Nashville to meet with them on Thursday evening at 6 p.m. I had paid through Saturday, but told the person that I would return. I was excited about sharing all that I had accomplished in my two months away. I packed everything on Wednesday evening. I woke at 2 a.m. the next morning and walked on the beach a bit listening to the waves as the moon shone on them. I hated to leave because this was such a peaceful place for my soul. But, I knew I must begin the 8-hour drive back to Nashville. I wanted to arrive early enough to take a nap and a shower before meeting with the UCC team. And, that is what I did.

That evening, I brought into the meeting my paintings, some of my journaling and my pictures. I was so excited to share the good things that had been happening in my soul and mind.

Right away, as I walked into the meeting room there was a weird static energy. I was told there wasn't time to look at my paintings. I did my best to share the good and renewing things I had been doing over the past two months. I felt over and over again that no one was really listening to me. There seemed to be a rush and anxiety for them to share and me to listen. And, they did—and I tried. But, my spirit was beginning to be crushed. All this amazing work I had done in the prior two months seemed to be dismissed.

I was reprimanded for not going to counseling. I had gone twice before I went to the beach for a month. And, I intended to return following my time at the beach. But, because I had not gone as often and, evidentially, had not gone to the "right person," there were some harsh concerns expressed. The chair of the team had the same emotional posture with me as had been present in the first surprise meeting. There was a condescension and disrespect as a fellow UCC minister that was not characteristic of the UCC that I knew and loved. I felt like I was being treated as "guilty" for something—and I had no idea what "it" was. I was not given a clue as to what was really going on, I just remember the static and negative energy that seem to pervade the room.

I was told that this team had spoken with 55 individuals from the congregation. Based on these conversations, the team was recommending that I take an additional 6 months sabbatical. I asked for clarity concerning the conversations with the 55 individuals. I was told they would meet with me at a later time and discuss this. For now, our time was up and we stood, held hands and prayed.

I gathered my paintings, pictures, and journals and was walking out of the room when one of the team informed me that he was going to escort me to my car. This seemed bizarre to me but the entire meeting was rather bizarre. So he took my paintings and I carried my bag and other things. It was dark as we walked into the parking lot. This man is over 6-feet tall. He hovered over me and in my personal space all the way to the car.

I have told other people when I recounted this experience that I felt like an inmate being escorted—all that were missing were handcuffs. The meeting filled me with guilt and shame, but

I was not given a reason as to why I should feel this way. It was the not being heard—almost feeling as if I were not acknowledged as a fellow human being. My worth and value were not really affirmed overall. Oh sure, words were spoken that seemed to give the appropriate and occasional "lip service" to me. But, they seemed obligatory and only used as a way to offset the negative energy filling the room and the judgments being made about me. There was no awareness that I had entered the meeting full of life and hope but was leaving feeling hopeless and disillusioned.

It wasn't until I got in my car and backed out of the parking lot and saw two Vestry members talking that I realized the reason I had been "escorted" to my car. Great effort was intentionally being exerted to keep me away from contact with anyone from the church. Something just wasn't right here but I had no idea at the time what "it" was.

I drove home and fell into Angie's arms crying and knowing something was very wrong, but there was absolutely nothing I could do about it.

Rev. Cyd Andrews-Looper

CHAPTER 39

You Want Me to What?

I texted the Vestry Chair the following day after the meeting with the UCC team. I was scheduled to be in the office the following Wednesday and preach the following Sunday. I was told to continue my sabbatical time. The Vestry was praying over the recommendations that the UCC team had made. She would let me know as soon as they had made a decision.

I thought surely by the middle of the following week, I would hear from her. It was two more weeks before she texted me to say that the Vestry wanted to meet with me. The fact that the Vestry had taken so long to "consider" the recommendations of the UCC team told me that there were things happening that were not right. All these discussions involved me, my life, and my ministry. Yet, I was not allowed to be a part of any of them. The very covenantal theology of the UCC was not being upheld.

When I walked into the small sanctuary of the church to meet with the Vestry, it was so good to see them. Even though we were meeting in the same space that the surprise blind-siding sin July had occurred, I was just glad to see familiar faces! The Vestry Chair had convinced me that they had good news to share with me—that they as a group were excited about sharing this good news with me. I walked in assuming I would be back in the pulpit the following Sunday. They were nice enough to look at my paintings, but there was a weird vibe going on among them.

They began asking me if I really thought I was ready to come back and preach. They questioned me to the point that I began to question my own readiness. Again, there seemed to be this negative energy that filled the room as they asked more and more negative questions and they gave me the impression that they thought the UCC team was out of touch with my ministry and our church. But, somehow they seemed to have the same weird energy I had felt with the UCC team.

The Vestry Chair called for a restroom break. When everyone returned, she basically "cut to the chase" and said, "Cindy, we have made a unanimous decision. We are asking you to resign."

Those words hit my heart and mind like a ton of bricks.

I said, "You are asking me to what??"

She repeated, "We have made a unanimous decision. We are asking you to resign."

I said, "What if I don't resign? What if instead, I ask for a congregational vote?" I knew that all UCC churches were autonomous and only the congregation could make this kind of decision.

Her response was, "Cindy, we have not felt the UCC has had your back. If you don't resign, they will make you go through a ministry fitness review and revoke your ordination. You will not have a future in ministry. We are trying to help you."

My mind and emotions in that moment were spinning so fast, I could hardly sit still but I had no reason to question what they were saying based on my experience with the UCC team. I actually thanked the Vestry members for loving me enough to have my back. I told them the only way I would resign was if I could tell the congregation in my own words. I told them I would assume responsibility for resigning. I would tell the congregation that God was leading me to a new chapter.

They said I could write the letter, but they wanted to approve it before it was sent out. I spent an entire day writing a long letter to this precious congregation and family I had known for 18 years. I cried throughout the day at the thought of leaving them.

A week after the letter went out, I was told my last Sunday would be October 5, 2014. This would also be the time that the congregation would say goodbye to me. A few days after my resignation email went out, the hopelessness that overwhelmed me was palpable. I began having suicidal thoughts. The pain I was feeling was unbearable. The shaming I had been through, yet without ever being told why I was being shamed. The losses I was facing. All of it was simply too much.

I began texting one of the Vestry telling her goodbye. I began texting Angie telling her goodbye as well. Angie had a knowing and intuition that was amazing. She was actually already on her way to our home when she read the suicidal thoughts in my texts.

When she arrived, she held me and told me I was not alone. She was going to be with me and walk with me through these moments. It wasn't long until two other church members showed up. Because I thought all that was happening was prompted by the UCC team, their presence was comforting to me. Never would I have dreamed that at the age of 51, I would be facing losses so great that suicide would appear to be a reasonable option—a relief from my pain.

Sunday, October 5 came quickly. This was the first time I had seen my dear church family and the first time I had been back inside the new sanctuary since my last sermon on July 20th. It was a very emotional time.

Angie sat close to me, along with two dear friends, Karen and Sally.

Karen and Sally are two women included on the dedication page of this book. They are there because, though they did not know me well at all; when I returned from sabbatical, they intentionally reached out to me. Sally sent me a very timely message from God on the same day I was having my most seriously suicidal thoughts. What developed from there was a close friendship, family presence, and support that have meant the world to me in my painful journey. They could see what I could not see. They have covered me with protective light and positive energy every day for many months. They have supported me financially in moments when I wasn't sure how things would be paid. They have been two of my biggest cheerleaders since I left Holy Trinity. Their presence with me, along with Angie, that last Sunday, was priceless.

The entire service was music. The staff had been kept in the dark about my return to the pulpit, so they planned something that would fill the Homecoming Service with a hopeful message.

I had asked if I could speak to the congregation and tell them goodbye. I was told that the question would be put to the Vestry, but I never received an answer. I have been told that some were informed that I did not want to speak to the congregation on that Sunday.

I would have given anything to tell my church family how much I loved them and how much I would miss them.

At the end of service, I was asked to come forward and stand at the altar table. I was not asked to come onto the platform, but to remain at the altar table for those who wanted to say goodbye. As I walked down the aisle, the entire congregation rose to their feet with resounding applause. When I arrived at the front, I looked deep into the eyes of as many people as I could, tears flowing down my cheeks, and held my hands over my heart.

I mouthed, "I love you" over and over again. I wanted more than ever for them to know that I indeed loved them with an everlasting love like a mother loves a child. I wanted to wrap my arms around each and every one there and tell them how much God loved them and to never forget their identity as a child of God.

But, I couldn't do that. I could only pray that my messages of hope had planted seeds within their hearts and minds. I could only hope and pray that they would always remember how valuable they were to God. I could only pray that God would hold them in the difficult days which lay ahead for them. They had no idea what was going on and they will probably never know the truth.

Angie, Karen, and Sally helped me pack my office on that Sunday afternoon. I had to drive away and try to not look back. I had to set my sights on my future. At 51 years old, I was having to start my life over from Ground Zero. I had no idea how difficult this new chapter would be and the unseen challenges that would arise. I had no idea that, literally, the darkest moments of my entire life lay ahead.

Rev. Cyd Andrews-Looper

CHAPTER 40

God's Love Is Always Present

During the last two weeks of my sabbatical, while I was at the beach, God told me that a condo would be available for me to purchase when I returned. There was a shell that caught my eye as I paused on the beach in those moments.

"This is your shell of promise," I sensed God saying to me. I picked it up. There wasn't anything special about it really. It wasn't very large, but it was perfectly formed. I kept that shell and have it framed today. I did return and purchased a condo which I closed on in mid-December.

After all that happened when I returned from sabbatical and was asked to resign, I fell into a deeply depressed emotional state. I had been having anxiety attacks since the beginning of 2014 and was prescribed meds for the times when they were particularly bad. I had also been experiencing mood swings that made me feel out of control. After leaving the church in October, the mood swings seemed to happen more frequently.

One of the challenges when I left was that I was informed that the church would only pay my health insurance through the end of October and I would have to get private health insurance in November. It hurt that the Vestry and Personnel Committee didn't care enough to keep me on the church insurance policy through the end of the year. I knew that the premiums for the fourth quarter had already been paid. I did not understand why they were going to such great lengths to cut me off completely. This additional financial stress did not help my emotionally fragile state. Thanks to ObamaCare, I was able to find insurance.

Following my last Sunday at Holy Trinity, Angie and I began having serious challenges. Honestly, the stress for both of us of her being my primary human contact while I was on sabbatical brought some unique dynamics to a very young relationship. I placed expectations on her that were unfair. And, she assumed responsibilities that were not hers to assume.

By the end of the year, the negative energy between us began feeling toxic. I told her that I didn't think I was really in a place emotionally to continue being in a relationship. And, she respected that. As we entered the New Year, the void of a support system in my life seemed overwhelming. It had been a natural occurrence for me to reach out and cling to her when I felt alone. I attempted to continue clinging to her. But, she had to draw an emotional line between us. It was very hard for me. It wasn't until February that I would realize just how hard. I know God was there because God's love is always there.

CHAPTER 41

Betrayal Can Kill You

I left Holy Trinity Community Church on October 5, 2014, I left not understanding what had happened during my two months away on sabbatical nor what happened during the 3 weeks following my meeting with the UCC team. So much didn't feel right or seem to add up. Because I was systematically kept from contact with the congregation and leadership during the sabbatical; and never given an opportunity to sit in a meeting that included the Vestry and UCC team, I can only believe that the plan was decided before I returned from sabbatical. I don't know specifically who planned it; but I believe the intention from the night I was blindsided by the surprise meeting to the meeting with the UCC team following the sabbatical, which was characterized by an awkward, condescending vibe, to the final meeting with the Vestry that filled a room with heaviness and dark energy, was to get rid of me.

I thought I would receive some kind of contact from the UCC team following the announcement that I had resigned. But, the fact that I did not receive any kind of call for pastoral care or concern speaks volumes, I believe. It was in late November 2014, when I had heard nothing from anyone in the Southeast

Conference of the UCC that I sent an email to the Conference Minister. We made plans to meet in mid-December.

Her mother passed in early December and we weren't able to meet until late January. It was at this meeting that I began getting a glimmer of the betrayal. She asked me how I was doing. I told her I was doing ok. That it had been hard to face leaving the church and being asked to resign. Her response was, "You were asked to resign?" I told her the story. I told her that when I told the Vestry that I was not going to resign, but instead ask for a congregational vote on their proposal—their response was if I did that the UCC would ask for a fitness review of my ministry and revoke my ordination. The Conference Minister then shared with me that she had asked the UCC team at every turn if anything they were finding rose to the level of a fitness review. And, their response every time was, "No."

She also said that my ordination was in place and I was in good standing.

I sat across from her in absolute shock. I told her that the Vestry had completely convinced me that the UCC was questioning my fitness for ministry and was going to revoke my ordination if I did not resign from the church.

She shook her head and apologized. She asked me if the UCC team had sat with me and actually talked through the report.

I told her the only meeting I had with them was the Thursday I returned from sabbatical.

She acknowledged that the UCC team had not done their due process in this very emotional and convoluted situation. She apologized for the disrespect and lack of care I had received from the UCC team. She had assumed they were being more pastoral in their approach with me.

I appreciated her pastoral presence and her willingness to listen in those moments.

Rev. Cyd Andrews-Looper

CHAPTER 42

A Season of Darkness and Despair

The news and awareness that the Vestry had lied to me in order to convince me to resign began an emotional spiraling that was difficult to fight. By mid-February, my emotional state was so hopeless that I had to check myself in to a psychiatric hospital. Angie was kind enough to drive me there and care for the puppy dogs I had to leave at home.

I could not handle the invisible—yet very real—boulder that was crushing my heart and soul as I realized the level of lies and betrayal which had occurred in the process of my leaving Holy Trinity. I had given my all to that church for 18 years and a handful of individuals apparently conspired to accomplish their task of getting rid of me. The staff had been led to believe that the UCC recommended that I resign. And, the congregation had been left in the dark the entire time.

When the UCC Team completed their report, the Vestry told the congregation that "since Pastor Cindy has resigned this report is now confidential and will remain so to protect Pastor Cindy." The impression was that I had done something terribly wrong, something seriously immoral.

I have been told that some individuals began leaving the church that day because they felt something just wasn't right about all that had happened. I have also heard that there was much speculation as to what I may have done. Cheat on Leigh with Angie? Take money from the church? Anyone who knew the structure of the church would have known that I had absolutely no access to any money—I didn't even know the code to the safe where the petty cash was kept— and anyone could have asked Leigh about rumors of my cheating and she would have put that to rest. We both let the other know before we began dating anyone else.

At every turn, my character had been vilified and I was given no opportunities to defend myself. Because of the UCC protocol for pastors who resign from churches, the expectation was that I would have no contact with anyone from the congregation. The reality was people were leaving the church and seeking me out. They wanted to know how I was doing and what in the world had happened.

The winter months were the most difficult for me. However, choosing to admit myself into the hospital was a wise decision. The psychiatrist was able to do the necessary evaluations. My diagnosis was Depression and ADHD with severe life changes and a loss of my stabilizing life systems. I was put on new meds and began weekly therapy sessions. I also followed up with my primary care physician.

The last time she had checked my labs for menopause was 2012. At that time, there was no indication that I was in menopause; even though I was within the age range. The labs that she took in March 2015 indicated that I had been in menopause about a year.

WOW!!!

That explained so much! I had not experienced the usual "hot flashes" that are the primary symptom of menopause. I also did not have a period because I had had an endometrial oblation in 2002. But, I had walked through an emotional fire storm and was in the midst of untreated menopause the entire time. My symptoms were mood swings—which I attributed primarily to the episodic events of the prior months—and occasional night sweats.

Clearly, being in the throes of menopause and going through so many losses made the mood swings more severe. It explained why I had so often teetered on suicidal thoughts. My primary care physician is a wonderfully compassionate and thorough practitioner. She put me on meds for menopause and followed up with me every two weeks to make sure I was responding well. Thankfully, my mood began to stabilize and a sense of well-being and hope were returning.

Rev. Cyd Andrews-Looper

CHAPTER 43

On Your Mark, Get Set, Launch!

On April 24, 2015, I officially launched **Ignite Your Soul Now** at GracePointe Church in Franklin, Tennessee. In January 2015, I had begun to attend this dynamic church which was struggling to truly live out the unconditional love of God by fully embracing the LGBTQ community. Stan Mitchell, the founding pastor, is a compassionate and incredibly gifted theologian in his own right. He is not only one of the most down-to-earth individuals I know but also, one of the most articulate teachers and preachers I have ever heard.

He faced losses of dear and close friends when he announced the full inclusion of the LGBTQ community but he stood with love, humility and grace. So much of his story and theology resonated with me. He became a friend and colleague—and also my pastor. I needed the love and support of community and the church family at GracePointe provided that for me.

I am thankful for Stan, Melissa, Paul, Ron, Carol, Kerri, Kim, Justin, Rachel, August and others who loved me when I needed it most.

I'm particularly thankful for six former Holy Trinity members who began attending GracePointe with me. They loved and supported me financially each month from February through May and helped me pay my basic bills for living.

Thank you! Rodney & Dave, Laurie & Lee Ann and Karen & Sally!

For the launch, I asked some dear friends and musicians to share their gifts. Thanks to Stephen Nix, Dan Ayers, Haley Baird, Erin Hardiman, Tim White, Cathy Wilder, Tim Causey, Leah Newman, Lisa Woodward, Sandy Flavin, Jason & DeMarco!

They did an amazing job and sang the perfect songs to create the positive energy and atmosphere that allowed me to share my heart and message. I was able to share my vision and lay out the plans for my writing, speaking, website and the new chapter that was unfolding before me.

It was an amazing time because, although I didn't know the "how" of everything, I knew with confidence that God had a plan of blessing for my future. From the launch, I had three additional individuals who began supporting me monthly, which helped tremendously.

A thanks to Beth & Amanda and Jimmy!

Seeing all the individuals who showed up to support me at the launch was so encouraging. Their love gave me new courage as I looked into my future. Many of them I had not seen since October 5, 2014.

I was surprised to see a former Vestry member who had been one of those asking me to leave. Part of me wondered if it was to "check up on me." Later, however, I discovered this person also had a sense that many things "were not right" in the handling of the events that followed the "surprise meeting" in July 2014. This person had left Holy Trinity in January and not returned. The picture of what actually happened was becoming clearer than ever.

CHAPTER 44

The Vote Must Be Unanimous

A couple of weeks following the launch of **Ignite Your Soul Now**, the former Vestry member reached out to me by saying, "Cindy, I would love to sit and talk with you. I believe you trusted some folks whom you thought had your back, but they didn't."

We met the following week and I shared my experience from the time of the surprise meeting until the launch of my new ministry. I explained that my fitness for ministry was never questioned by the UCC and my ordination was in good standing.

This former Vestry member was quite shocked at this news. It seems the Vestry Chair and another Vestry member, along with a Personnel Committee member felt strongly that I should be asked to resign but not all of the Vestry members agreed. The Vestry Chair shared at each meeting that she was in close contact with the Chair of the UCC team. In such close contact that she said jokingly, "He and I are becoming best friends."

At the last Vestry meeting before they were to have with me, the Vestry Chair shared that she had talked at length with the UCC Team Chair and the Conference Minister. Both, she said, told her if the Vestry could not convince me to resign, I would have to go through a fitness review, and my ordination would be revoked. The Vestry Chair presented this information with seeming concern for me and the future of my ministry. She convinced those Vestry members who were not willing to vote in favor of asking me to resign that a unanimous vote was needed. She explained that the Vestry needed to be of one mind on this so that they could communicate to me that the vote was unanimous.

When the former Vestry member realized that the Vestry Chair had flat out lied to the Vestry as a whole in order to get a unanimous vote, she was visibly angered. It was then the former Vestry member began recounting events over the prior two years in which the Vestry Chair and another Vestry member had undermined my leadership when I was not present.

Surprisingly for me, this news was somewhat of a relief. Though it did not explain the motive, it at least explained how things happened before the surprise meeting and all the events that followed. There had been for some time an undercurrent of negativity toward me from these two individuals. These same two individuals had served on the Personnel Committee in prior years. The events that unfolded from June 2014-October 2014, simply provided ample opportunities to force the founding pastor from the church and that is basically what happened. From here, I began researching pastors who had been forced out of their churches. What I discovered was mind boggling.

CHAPTER 45

Forced Terminations

In the late spring of 2015, I began reading about forced terminations of clergy. What I discovered was that it is an event that happens far too often. Approximately one-third of current clergy have or will experience being forced from their church.

The impact that this has on the person emotionally, financially, mentally, and spiritually is enormous. It has brought talented and effective pastors to the point of suicide. It has left pastors and their families out on the street to fend for themselves.

It is so prevalent that, in 1994, Dr. Charles Chandler started the Ministering to Ministers Foundation. Today he serves as the Executive Director of this non-denominational organization whose sole purpose is to support, care for, counsel, and renew clergy who have been forced out of their churches. His website shares some of his experience and quotes an article by David Goetz in which Goetz identified three "dynamic" patterns in similar occurrences.

(David L. Goetz, "Forced Out," Leadership, (Carol Stream, IL: Volume XVII Number 1, Winter 1996) p.42)

First, each minister had been "blind-sided." A group of two or three persons—usually self-appointed—approached the minister without warning and said he or she should resign because they had lost their effectiveness. They convinced the minister that the whole church shared their feeling. The "group" presented themselves as merely "messengers" and insisted there was nothing personal about the request. The messengers told the minister they loved him or her and really hated to deliver the resignation request.

Second, while the minister was in a state of shock after being blindsided, the "group" dumped guilt on the minister. They said the resignation and related conversation must be kept very quiet. If word got out, it could split the church and the minister would not want to be known as one who caused a split church! Any negative effect from the minister's departure was dumped directly on him or her as though a minister could just slip away and never be missed.

Third While the minister was still in no condition to make a decision of any kind, the group pressed for a decision. In most cases, a few weeks or a few months of severance was offered—provided the resignation was given immediately and the entire negotiation was kept secret. The "messengers" added, "We have to know what you plan to do, because if you refuse to resign, or if you talk to other church members, we will take away the severance, and call a church business meeting to fire you. Then you will get nothing."

At this point, Goetz says he has decided a rulebook is floating around out there somewhere and it suggests that a few disgruntled church members can follow these rules and "kick the preacher out." He's never seen it in writing, but its effectiveness can be seen in case after case.

Goetz suggests looking at some of the fallacies and undesirable ethics endorsed by this phantom rulebook. Though the "messengers" present themselves as representing the vast majority of the membership, according to a survey conducted by Leadership magazine, 43 percent of forced-out ministers said a "faction" pushed them out, and 71 percent of those stated that the "faction" numbered 10 persons or less. The self-appointed "messengers" often hoard the inside information to themselves, because only 20 percent of the forced out ministers said the real reason for their leaving was made known to the entire congregation.

Goetz is convinced the typical statement that warns the minister to remain quiet or risk losing severance money translates as, "We do not have the votes to remove the minister via a church vote." Ministers often remain quiet because they are afraid to take a chance on having nothing with which to house and feed their families. A significant number of ministers have no savings due to inadequate salaries. They often fall victim to the "group's" argument that remaining quiet is taking the "high road." Disclosing this secret may be painful, but it is the only way a church is able to stay or become healthy.

Rev. Cyd Andrews-Looper

CHAPTER 46

Pastors, Take Care of Yourselves!

As I look over the last 18 years of my ministry, it truly seems like a lifetime. I have learned many lessons. I have preached many sermons, taught many classes, said many prayers, consecrated the communion elements many times, baptized many souls, both adults and children, dedicated many infants, married many couples, both straight and gay, sat by the bedside of many dying members, preached many funerals, some very sad and others that were true celebrations, sat and listened to so many souls as they shared stories of abuse and brokenness, cried with those who were hurting from losses.

Honestly, I have pushed myself for years above and beyond for the sake of the church. I don't say this begrudgingly. For those of you who pastors growing your churches, you know that it is an incredibly exciting journey but a stressful one. The pushing onward and upward and keeping a stiff upper lip in the face of exhaustion is what I have known for many years.

It is easy when you found a church—or pastor a small church that experiences significant growth quickly—for the church to be built around you. This is difficult to avoid because it becomes like your baby and, you will give sacrificially, of yourself for the sake of this church. Pastoring a church through periods of growth can be very stressful. You start out as the only pastor who knows everyone attending the church. Then, more people start coming and there are more people to which you can effectively keep up.

You know you need more pastoral staff to help you, but you think you can manage one more budget year and, in that year, you have unexpected deaths in the congregation that weigh on your heart. You have people complaining that you are ignoring them—when you feel like you are doing well to barely keep up with the serious pastoral care needs that are coming your way. You have people complaining about the crowded conditions of worship and you plow onward with a smile, hoping relief will come in time.

If you are a pastor reading this and leading a growing organization, please take care of yourself physically, emotionally, and spiritually. You are called to carry the burdens of many in your congregation; to be attentive to what God is calling you to preach each week—even when you know it is going to step on some toes—to be on call 24/7 because the phone could ring in the middle of the night or just as you have received your food in a restaurant. Through all of this, you have to put on a smile and act like all is well even though you may be facing serious personal challenges. Because you live in a "fishbowl," you are accustomed to putting on a smile and happy face no matter what is going on.

The people who follow you seldom see or recognize the challenges or pain that you may be facing. It is your responsibility as a leader to recognize and ask for the time you need for rest and renewal. Your ability to lead effectively will depend on it. Surround yourself with people with whom you can be vulnerable and honest and let them be your advocates. Use the resources and recommendations of your denomination concerning self-care. Your Sabbath time as a spiritual leader is one of the most important disciplines in your ministry. Practice it and keep it safe and don't feel guilty or apologize for taking time away. In order for God to use you, you have to be a healthy vessel.

Don't ever compromise this piece of the puzzle!

Pastoring was a job I loved but it was also the hardest job that I have ever had. It is a lonely place that only another pastor can understand. I believe part of my ministry moving forward is to love and encourage other pastors who are on the front line. I will remind you that you are doing kingdom work. Nothing you do in the name of love will be in vain. Know that just as God called you, so also God will give you the strength and grace to lead the flock. But, please take care of yourselves!

If you are a part of the leadership in a church, please take care of your pastor. Make sure he or she is taking time away on a regular schedule. Build into their compensation a sabbatical that allows them time off with no expectations. They need this to stay refreshed and able to lead effectively.

One area in which I failed myself and the Holy Trinity congregation was in not standing up for myself. I should have asked for denominational support in negotiating a proper sabbatical. By not having time for renewal, I allowed myself to get burned out beyond a healthy capacity to function and when significant aspects of the relationship broke up, I lacked a healthy perspective in how best to respond. My response caused unrest and instability among the congregation. It provided the perfect storm for a small group to accomplish their ultimate mission. The firestorm included Facebook postings of personal email, false accusations and rumors, lies told to staff and leadership, and the congregation deliberately kept in the dark.

If I had not been in such an emotionally compromised and exhausted place, I know I would have had a healthier perspective following the announcement that Leigh and I made and provided a much healthier response.

Hindsight is always 20/20. The lessons I have learned over the past year have been significant. Most have related to the awareness of my own needs in regard to staying in a healthy place emotionally and mentally. Today I practice a number of disciplines which keep my mind calm and my soul renewed. I live with greater awareness and mindfulness daily.

CHAPTER 47

The Heartbeat of my Message

My life journey has taken many twists and turns. I have experienced amazing blessings on the mountaintop of life. Blessings in which I stood in awe of God's goodness and love but I have also experienced some of the darkest valleys that brought me to despair and suicide. The one stabilizing and consistent presence throughout has been my relationship with God. It has been that unconditional love that has carried me and given me peace in the darkest of nights. I have realized that my greatest title and accomplishment in this life is simply Beloved Child of God.

I did not, nor would I have, come to this realization from the legalistic faith of my childhood. Those rules simply reinforced fear and an inadequacy before God. It has been getting to know Jesus Christ on a deeper level and studying His teachings and life that have helped me claim my rightful identity as a Beloved Child of God eternally loved by my Creator, Redeemer, and Sustainer.

In Matthew 22:37-40, Jesus says,

> "Love the Lord your God with all your heart and with all your soul and with all your mind. This is the first and greatest command. And the second is like it: 'Love your neighbor as yourself.' All the Law and the Prophets hang on these two commandments."

Many ministers begin, when teaching this passage, with "Love the Lord your God..." but I begin at the end of the second command. Those two words: "as yourself." Those two words are loaded with potential and truth. Until we know and see ourselves as a Beloved Child of God, there will be little stability in our spiritual and emotional life and we cannot know or understand ourselves as a Beloved Child of God until we see God as love—love and nothing else.

I John 4:8 tells us that, "God is love." Legalisms blind us to this eternal truth. Legalistic rules reinforce the concept of God as the Great Judge in the Sky ready to pounce on and condemn us at every turn. No one wants to or can get close to a God like that because the very thought of God as a Judge fills us with fear.

How can we see ourselves as Beloved Children of God if we are filled with fear at the very thought of God?

How can we love God, ourselves or our neighbor if we see God as this Judge ready to condemn us for nor keeping "the rules?"

The reality is we can't and we don't.

My observations and experiences have proven that there really is no middle ground when it comes to love. We either believe and embrace God as love or we make an attempt to please God by keeping the rules. The rules may bring us comfort on occasion when we feel we are "keeping them." but that comfort is short-lived because we were not made to keep rules.

We were made to know, receive, live, and give love in this world. When we do, we are connecting with the infinite power and love of the God who created thousands of universes. Love always wins in the end.

Look at the life of Jesus. He taught love and lived love. He angered those who held fast to the rules. They became so angry, in fact that they conspired successfully to have Him crucified.

Remember that there is no power on earth or heaven that can overcome love. Thus, three days later, love was resurrected.

My faith today is defined by love alone. I cannot add to or take from it. It has been in my willingness to relinquish "the rules" and seek love that I have found peace and hope. Even in the darkest nights, there has been an abiding Presence and Love that has sustained me. It has been the God of eternal love who claims me as the Beloved Child.

Out of that intimate relationship has grown a passion to share this powerful truth.

I have seen truth transform lives that were broken and restore them to wholeness and peace.

Love is the only answer for your life and for this world.

My challenge is learning to love those who continue the harsh judgments by holding fast to the rules of their faith. What God's love has revealed to me is that these individuals simply live and teach what they know. They know religious rules. They know fear. From that place, the only next step is to hold others to this place of bondage but they are simply believing what they have been taught and doing their best.

When I understand and see these, my brothers and sisters, as Beloved Children of God and know that they are caught in the trap of fear, my deep desire is to share my message of hope and love. I want them to find the peace and hope which I have found.

And, that is my desire for you as well.

My dear sister or brother, you cannot see yourself as a Beloved Child of God until you know and believe that God is love and nothing more. When you see God, your Creator, Redeemer, and Sustainer, as love you automatically see yourself as a beautiful and loved child and, when you see yourself in this truth, you can't help but live that out.

The love simply oozes from your being.

The "loving your neighbor as yourself" requires little thought because the mighty and powerful love of God is in you and flowing through you. That kind of love changes the world. It changes the church. That kind of love ignites your soul and puts you in touch with the home of your soul: the unseen spiritual realm that has no limits in love or abundance.

My prayer for you,

My prayer for the church,

My prayer for the world, is that we simply relinquish the religious rules and lie back in the abounding love of God and claim our rightful identity as a Beloved Child of God!

> "See what great love God has lavished on us, that we should be called children of God. And that is what we are!" I John 3:1

CHAPTER 48

Discovering New Light and New Truth

I have been a seeker of truth all my life. It is this desire to find truth that has allowed me to embrace new truths that cross my path and it has been this new light and truth that allowed me to accept my call into ministry as a woman. It is this new light and truth that allowed me to reconcile my faith and sexual orientation. I no longer fear new light or truth.

At the beginning of 2013, I began praying and asking God to show me new light and truth—not just truth and light as defined by my Christian faith but truth and light that was greater than any single religion.

I began slowly to open myself to learning from other faiths. I began studying and reading about the laws of the universe. Of particular interest to me was the law of attraction, the law of vibrational frequencies, and the law of intent.

The more I studied these laws and understood them, the more I realized that they were also understood and taught by Jesus. Jesus' teaching of sowing and reaping parallels the law of attraction. Jesus teachings on love parallels the law of vibrational frequencies since love holds the highest vibrational frequency that we can experience in our physical body. Jesus' teachings and the New Testament instruction on the focus of our thoughts parallels the law of intent.

Studying these truths, learning to meditate and center myself in a peaceful place…learning to be still and quiet my soul helped me realize the power of the unseen spiritual realm. It has given me new light to share with the world. The more I learn about the universal laws, the greater my passion is to share this truth, light, and love.

As part of my own journey, I became a certified trainer for Mike Dooley's **Infinite Possibilities** program. My journey has stirred new excitement in my soul. It has allowed me to get in touch with the powerful Spirit of the unseen realm. My understanding of God has broadened greatly. My understanding of myself and others as eternal spiritual beings having a physical experience on earth has helped me understand why I am here.

In my meditating and connection with God, I have realized that humanity has forgotten what our souls have never forgotten. We have forgotten that we are first and foremost spiritual beings having a physical experience. We have become so engaged in the physical experience that we have developed amnesia about the spiritual realm. We have forgotten that the physical experience is just an illusion. We have embraced it as reality. Everything about our physical experience is finite and limited.

We live our lives from a mindset of lack, instead of abundance. This has caused much fear and anxiety to rise up within our souls. The only way to eradicate the anxiety and fear is to remember.

Remember that we are eternal, infinite spiritual beings eternally loved by God who are having a physical experience.

Remember that the spiritual realm is what is real and true.

Remember that the life and hope we seek will be found by engaging the spiritual, unseen realm.

Remember that quietness and stillness are required to engage the infinite spiritual realm.

Remember that the anxiety and fear we feel are symptoms of our spiritual amnesia.

The more I sit still and quietly listen, the more a passion rises up within me to share these powerful truths that so many have forgotten. For those who are learning and embracing these truths, there is a greater awareness that we are part of the Kingdom of God being built on the earth. A daily stillness allows our souls to connect with God, the Source of all that is. A daily stillness helps us understand that there is a unity and oneness in all of creation that is held together by a holy love.

I am thankful for the new light and truth that is rising up within my soul. My desire is to proclaim it and live it in such a way that there is a fullness of light and love in this world that overwhelms any darkness that may lurk in the unknown and hidden cavities of our physical world.

We are co-creators, with God, of light and love.

We choose, daily, what we will attract into our lives and what we are producing with our efforts.

We are all on this physical journey together but the physical experience is an illusion.

We must live this physical experience by the greater laws of the spirit. This allows us to live out our birthright of abundance as children of God.

I want to remind every soul I touch that they are Beloved Children of God, wholly loved and full of light. I want to use my light and my connection to God to help ignite the souls who have lost hope.

I continue to be still

…and quiet

…and listen.

I continue to open my heart and mind to truth and ask God to use me to impart this truth for good in the world.

Rev. Cyd Andrews-Looper

CHAPTER 50

What's Next?

I hope you will stay tuned to hear about the next chapter. As I write these words, I am filled with great love and thanksgiving. A love so great that, even the pain and anger from the wrongs and betrayals which occurred in the past have melted away.

I believe, on some level, that those who orchestrated my exit were doing the best that they knew how in handling a very complicated situation. I've realized that it was indeed time for me to move from the parish ministry at Holy Trinity.

I find myself in a place of giving sincere thanks to God. I'm beginning to see the openhanded blessings that are starting to unfold in this new chapter of my life.

I see now that God used a difficult situation to move me from a place that was no longer part of the Divine plan of my life.

As I move fully into this new chapter of my life and a new ministry, I am not certain the form it will take but I believe that the excitement that I feel when I think about it means it will be good.

My past experiences with God have proven that God blesses me openhandedly when I am willing to obey and it seems that the bigger the steps of faith, the greater the blessings that follow.

So, I am looking into my future with anticipation. I believe God is in the process of doing something amazing and I don't want to miss it!

Wherever you are right now, whether you are walking through the fire, trying to find your way in the darkness, or in the midst of great celebration, I encourage you to keep God in the pictures and events of your life. I remind you that God is your loving Creator. God, who spoke the moon, the sun and the stars of millions of universes into place, created you with purpose. When you are living from the purpose for which you were created, you have amazing joy and satisfaction; and love flows through you so freely.

If you are reading these words and don't feel like your life has meaning or purpose, I invite you to join me in my journey.

God wants to ignite your soul now!

You have dreams that you think have died but my brother or sister, God wants to resurrect those dreams. You may be reading this, and like me, thinking you are "too old" to change careers, go back to school, buy a house, move to another state, start painting, record an album, open a restaurant or anything else

I don't know what your dream is but if you are reading this, it is not by accident! God is using this book and this message to light the fire within you once again.

Whether you are 35 or 75, please don't let your dream die with you.

I will be your cheerleader.

Come to my website and start following me. We will make this journey together. God is not finished with you yet. When you close this book or turn off your e-reader, please get a pen and paper, and make a list of ten things you need to do to revive your dream.

It may be to make phone calls or send emails. It may be getting online and doing some research. It may be going to a college and getting an application to enroll. It may be making a menu for a restaurant you want to open.

Whatever it is, don't let the enemy try to scare you away from your dreams! He has obviously succeeded before.

Stop living from this place of fear.

God has a plan for you!

That plan is to make you prosper, it is not to harm you. That plan is to give you hope and a future. It is time to stop living in fear and start living in hope!

Please make sure you include me on your list of ten things to do. Send me an email and start following me. I will walk with you. I will pray with you. I will remind you that God is the ever-present Source of all that is and is certainly not finished with you yet. I'll remind you that God is abundant love and that your life is about to change in an amazing way!

I can't wait to hear YOUR story!

My website is: www.igniteursoulnow.org

E-mail me at: igniteursoulnow@gmail.com

Facebook: www.facebook.com/cynthia.andrewslooper

Instagram: Igniteursoulnow Twitter: @igniteursoulnow

I'm waiting to hear from you!

Remember, LOVE wins, Rev. Cyd

Rev. Cyd Andrews-Looper

APPENDIX

The intent of this appendix is to explain in "laymen's terms" some of the foundational issues related to reconciling one's faith and sexual orientation. It is not meant to be scholarly. But, instead to give a framework from which one can begin to understand the process of finding peace. This is from a class I teach called, "Bullying from the Pulpit."

On the issue of homosexuality and scripture, bullying from the pulpit happens when scripture is misinterpreted. Misinterpretation occurs when scripture passages that were written thousands of years ago are interpreted literally in the 21st century.

There are two primary ways of interpreting scripture: literally or historically-critically. Literal interpretation reads a text and interprets it verbatim within a particular contemporary culture. Historical-critical interpretation sheds the light of culture on the passage. It asks who wrote this? To whom was it written? When was it written? Why was it written? What was the significance of it within the culture in which it was written?

Example of how literal interpretation causes misinterpretation:

Some Chinese college students come to America and spend some time with American students at a local university. The Chinese students know English well enough to converse with the American students. However, they aren't entirely familiar with our culture.

Each day the two groups of students get together and discuss the topic that is being studied. One day, the American group is talking about one of their members. One of the American students says, "She's out in left field." As Americans, we know exactly what is meant by that statement. However, the Chinese students don't understand and they take the statement literally. They become very concerned that one of their American friends is stuck out in the left side of a field. They want to go look for her and help her. When the American students realize what is happening, they explain to the Chinese students that "she's out in left field" is an idiom of our culture and language based on the diagram of players in a baseball game. The left fielder appears so far out that he or she is disconnected from what is going on in the game. However, because most batters are right handed, it is necessary for the left fielder to play deep in the left field.

From here, the American students would explain that this is a statement made of someone who seems disconnected from what is really going on in a given situation. In this example, the American students had to allow the cultural light to shine on this statement in order for it to be correctly understood by the Chinese students.

In like manner, when we interpret scriptural texts literally, we come to inaccurate conclusions of what the passage is actually saying. Only by allowing the cultural and historical light to shine on a passage can we come to the most accurate understanding of what the passage means.

There are six verses in scripture that are used to condemn gay and lesbian relationships. The verses are interpreted literally without the understanding of their historical and cultural background.

When we look at these verses through the historical-critical lens of interpretation, we come to the conclusion very quickly that what is being condemned has nothing to do with what we know today as two people of the same gender being in a loving, committed relationship.

When we look at the six passages used to condemn the LGBTQ community, there are three primary reasons that homo-genital acts are condemned in scripture:

1) Pagan worship,
2) Humiliation of males via rape,
3) Abusive relationships between older men and young boys.

In none of the six scripture passages is there a reference or understanding to what we know today as two people of the same gender being in a loving, committed relationship.

An additional note concerning these verses:

The status of women in ancient Hebrew culture was very low; barely above that of children and slaves. When a man engaged in sexual intercourse with a woman, he always took a dominant position, as penetrator; the woman took the submissive posture. When two men engaged in sexual intercourse, one of the men, in effect, takes the role of a woman. When a man takes on the low status of a woman, the act makes both ritually impure. (It was considered an abomination for a man to be treated like a woman).

http://www.religioustolerance.org/hom_bibh5.htm

These are the six passages used to condemn the LGBTQ community:

Leviticus 18:22

"'Do not have sexual relations with a man as one does with a woman; that is detestable.

It is interesting to see how this chapter begins:

The LORD said to Moses, "Speak to the Israelites and say to them: 'I am the LORD your God. You must not do as they do in Egypt, where you used to live, and you must not do as they do in the land of Canaan, where I am bringing you. Do not follow their practices."

It seems normal to want to know and understand what the "practices of those in Egypt and Canaan" were. When we look at the culture of these two areas, we see pagan worship and practices very prevalent. In particular, worship of Ashtar, the fertility goddess. Sexual activity is how her followers worshiped her. Men seeking to worship her sought out in particular, the *galli*. These were greatly valued and honored men who had castrated themselves (penis and testicles) for the goddess. They literally sacrificed their masculinity to serve the goddess. They embraced the femininity of the goddess by dressing as a woman. The *galli* were considered to be particularly holy. Male worshipers worshiped the fertility goddess by having anal sex with the *galli*. There were women who served as temple prostitutes, but did not have the honor or value that the *galli* held.

http://www.whiterockchurch.org/wrcc/teaching/educati on/homosexuality/archapter2.html

Leviticus 20:13

"'If a man has sexual relations with a man as one does with a woman, both of them have done what is detestable."

This chapter begins giving warning for anyone who sacrifices their child to the god, Molek. Ashtar or Ishtar, the fertility goddess that we have just discussed, was also the feminine cohort of Molek. Then what follows is a list similar to Leviticus 18.

In verse 22-23 of Leviticus 20, Moses says the following:

"'Keep all my decrees and laws and follow them, so that the land where I am bringing you to live may not vomit you out. You must not live according to the customs of the nations I am going to drive out before you. Because they did all these things, I abhorred them."

It is clear that God wanted His people to be distinctly separate from the inhabitants of Egypt or Canaan. The prevailing influence in both cultures was paganism.

Additionally, in some paraphrases and translations of the Bible, the word "homosexuality" is used in Leviticus 18:22 and 20:13. It is interesting to note that this word was not introduced into the Bible until 1946. By using this word, it automatically created a blanket condemnation for the LGBTQ community.

Genesis 19 –Story of Sodom and Gomorrah

This story is simply about rape and male humiliation. Several cultural points to consider:

1. This culture, found in the desert where people could easily die when traveling, had a sacred obligation of hospitality. Deeply imbedded was the obligation that one was to provide shelter for strangers and those needing a safe place to stay overnight.

2. All men of the town (this obviously includes men married to women and very heterosexual) want to "know" the strangers—they are seeking to rape them and humiliate them by treating them like women.

3. Lot offered his daughters who were, in effect, his property, to the men. Culturally it was better to give away your daughter/property than to allow dishonor of a male guest in your home.

> "unconcerned; they did not help the poor and needy. They were haughty and did detestable things before me.
> Therefore I did away with them as you have seen."

I Corinthians 6:9-10
"Or do you not know that wrongdoers will not inherit the kingdom of God? Do not be deceived: Neither the sexually immoral nor idolaters nor adulterers nor men who have sex with men nor thieves nor the greedy nor drunkards nor slanderers nor swindlers will inherit the kingdom of God."

I Timothy 1:9-11
"We also know that the law is made not for the righteous but for lawbreakers and rebels, the ungodly and sinful, the unholy and irreligious, for those who kill their fathers or mothers, for murderers, for the sexually immoral, for those practicing homosexuality, for slave traders and liars and perjurers—and for whatever else is contrary to the sound doctrine that conforms to the gospel concerning the glory of the blessed God, which he entrusted to me."

These two verses are highly debated by scholars. This is because there are two Greek words (*arsenokoitai* & *malakoi*) which are very unclear as we attempt to understand their cultural reference.

The difficulty in interpreting these words is because:

1. They are simply supplied in a listing of ancient literature without a context in which to put them. Additionally, one of the words (*arsenkoitai*) is only used in the Bible in these two verses.

2. The interpretation of these words has changed from generation to generation as prejudices of the day change. Each interpretation offers the "opinion of the day" with no real certainty of the words and their use to the text to condemn same sex relationships.

3. *Malakoi* has been translated through the years, depending on the culture, as masturbators, homosexuals, sexual perverts, male prostitutes, the effeminate.

The literal translation of *malakoi* is "soft." (It is also the word used in Matthew 11:18 to describe fine clothing). Possible interpretations when applied to moral matters:

a) loose, wanton, lewd, lustful, unrestrained (Boswell);
b) effeminate call boys (Scroggs).

4. *Arsenkoitai* has been translated through the years, depending on the culture, as homosexuals, sexual perverts, sodomites, child molesters, practicing homosexuals

The literal translation of *arsenkoitai* is "man-sleeper" or "man-penetrator." (Be mindful that words do not always mean what the literal translation states. Example: "lady killer") Possible interpretations:

a) male prostitutes (Boswell);
b) older man who sleeps with young call boys (Scroggs);
c) some kind of economic exploitation by sexual means such as prostitution or pimping (Martin)

5. Consideration: Just as biblical opposition to prostitution, incest or adultery does not forbid straight

(heterosexual) sex, so also biblical opposition of abuse, prostitution, lewd, wanton, or exploitive sex does not forbid gay (homo-genital) sex.

As the author of this book, I recognize the challenges of these two verses. However, present within the culture or that time were older men who sought out younger call boys with whom to have sex. It was known as pederasty. The closest thing within our 21st century culture is pedophilia. This activity is something that we condemn. However, that behavior does not speak in any way of two people of the same gender being in a loving, committed relationship.

The conclusion we come to after interpreting these "clobber passages" historically-critically is not one speaks of our understanding of "gay relationships" and gay marriages.

Another important point is Jesus, our Redeemer and the Cornerstone of our Christian faith, said nothing about homosexual acts. I believe this is true because His focus was love alone and I believe this is the lens through which we must evaluate all relationships: love alone.

"And now these three remain: faith, hope and love. But the greatest of these is love."
I Corinthians 13:13

A MODERN DAY PARABLE CONCERNING CULTURAL NORMS

This is a true story which illustrates how something can be interpreted as "bad" in one cultural and "good" in another.

I have a dear friend, Lynne, who is married to a minister. They are originally from North Carolina. In the early 90's, Bill felt called to move to Los Angeles to start a church. They packed up their belongings and their five year old daughter, Bethany, and moved to the gang-ridden city of LA. They very quickly realized just how prevalent the gangs were and the rivalries present between the most violent gangs. The two most dangerous, violent, and rival gangs at that time were the Bloods and the Crips.

In the fall, they enrolled Bethany in first grade. They were amazed when they received the student handbook of all the restrictions listed in what the students could wear and not wear. There were particular symbols, clothing patterns and colors that children were forbidden to wear. This was because these symbols, clothing patterns and colors were identified with the different gangs. To wear any of these could potentially put the children in harm's way.

The symbol for the Bloods was a red bandana. Bethany learned very quickly that anyone wearing a red bandana was part of one of the most dangerous and violent gangs in her new city. Her parents always assured her that God would always protect her. But, the impression this child had of red bandanas was formed entirely by her experience of living in a culture permeated by gangs.

The following July, Bill, Lynne & Bethany, made a visit back home to North Carolina over the 4th of July. They attended a big cookout at Lynne's parent's house and had many friends and family there to see them. However, they never anticipated what was going to happen when they arrived with Bethany.

Lynne's mother was dressed in a jean skirt, crisp white blouse and a red bandana around her neck. Bethany loved her "Nana" dearly and could not wait to see her. Nana had spoiled her well when she was very young and lived in North Carolina.

However, when Bethany saw her grandmother wearing a red bandana, the child literally went hysterical.

She began screaming, "No, no, no!!! Nana, is not bad! Nana is not mean! No, no, no!"

Bill had to pick her up and take her inside and calm her down. It was there that he had to explain that red bandanas are not good or bad but, when mean people wear them, we could think anyone who wears them is also bad. He had to explain that when someone wears a red bandana in LA, they are identifying with the gang, the Bloods. However, there were no Bloods in North Carolina. So, when people wore a red bandana in North Carolina, it did not mean they were mean people. They just liked red bandanas.

This seemed to help some but, as you can imagine, Lynne's mother felt horrible and removed the red bandana.

Bill took the red bandana and wore it himself to let Bethany know that red bandanas are not good or bad. But, depending on the cultural context, they could be perceived as bad.

In many ways, I believe the blanket condemnation of the LGBTQ community based on the six "clobber passages" is like condemning "Nana" because she was wearing a red bandana. The clobber passages are condemning homo-genital acts based on specific cultural norms which are not present in our 21st culture. Additionally, there was no understanding as we have today that an individual can be born with a natural attraction to the same gender.

As Dr. Ralph Blair, President of Evangelicals Concerned, says, "The Bible is an empty closet when it comes to gay and lesbian relationships."

We cannot and should not use scripture to abuse our brothers and sisters under any circumstances. To do so is being a spiritual bully and far removed from what Jesus calls us to do.

Simply put, we must live by the law of love. Nothing else is simpler or more powerful.

Love always wins! Always!

Made in the USA
Lexington, KY
22 March 2018